This book generously donated by
Roy and Robert Marsh
in celebration of
Milo Hamilton

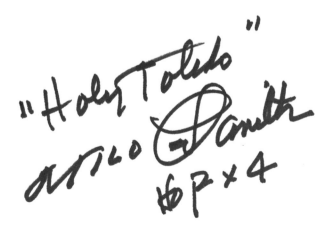

"Holy Toledo"
Milo Hamilton
HOF x 4

MAKING AIRWAVES

60 Years at Milo's Microphone

MILO HAMILTON
AND DAN SCHLOSSBERG
WITH BOB IBACH

SportsPublishingLLC.com

ISBN: 1-59670-027-0

Publishers: Peter L. Bannon and Joseph J. Bannon Sr.
Senior managing editor: Susan M. Moyer
Acquisitions editor: Bob Snodgrass
Developmental editor: Doug Hoepker
Photo editor: Erin Linden-Levy
Art director: K. Jeffrey Higgerson
Dust jacket design: Kenneth J. O'Brien
Interior layout design: Kathryn R. Holleman
Imaging: Dustin Hubbart, Kathryn R. Holleman

Printed in the United States of America

Sports Publishing L.L.C.
804 North Neil Street
Champaign, IL 61820

Phone: 1-877-424-2665
Fax: 217-363-2073
SportsPublishingLLC.com

    Library of Congress Cataloging-in-Publication Data
Hamilton, Milo, 1927-
    Making airwaves : 60 years at Milo's microphone / Milo Hamilton and Dan Schlossberg with Bob Ibach.
        p. cm.
    Includes index.
    ISBN 1-59670-027-0 (hardcover : alk. paper)
    1. Hamilton, Milo, 1927- 2. Sportscasters—United States—Biography. I. Schlossberg, Dan, 1948- II. Ibach, Bob. III. Title.

    GV742.42.H355A3 2006
    070.4'49796092—dc22
                    2005033234

To Arlene, my love and inspiration,
in appreciation for 53 terrific years of
friendship, laughter, and encouragement.

—M.H.

CONTENTS

FOREWORD

BY NOLAN RYAN

Milo Hamilton and I have something in common: longevity. To have longevity, you have to have good health, be dedicated, and have a passion for what you do. You have to be able to maintain what it requires of you, so I think it's a reflection of where Milo is, how he feels about the game, and what he does. He takes a lot of pride in his job.

He has a passion for what he does and for the game. That's the reason he has accomplished what he has. You just don't find people who are able to do that too often.

Just as preparation is the key to success for a player, it's the same thing for a broadcaster. When you listen to Milo's broadcasts, you can tell he's prepared. That's why he has such insight to what's going on with the team. The unique thing about a radio broadcaster is that he follows the club on a daily basis. Listeners look for that person to paint the picture every day and bring in all that information so they feel like they truly are in touch with the ballclub.

Milo can do TV or radio but I know he thinks radio is the best fit for him, his style, and what he enjoys doing.

When he got into the broadcast wing of the Baseball Hall of Fame, I thought it was appropriate that he be recognized in that light because of his love, compassion, and commitment for the game. That comes across in his broadcasts. To be able to keep up the grind like Vin Scully, Jack Buck, and some of those guys, it was only appropriate he be recognized in that manner.

I actually met Milo when he was with the Cubs. But our friendship started developing when he came to Houston when I was with the Astros. With baseball, you meet people from other organizations, through the media especially, just through association with the game. But we became friends when we worked together with the Astros.

We have a common interest in hunting. When we'd have lunch together, Milo would tell me that he used to go quail hunting on some of those old Georgia plantations during the years he was with Atlanta. The first time we went quail hunting together came after he had received the Astro of the Year award from a radio station in Corpus Christi; he had a large following down there.

The prize turned out to be a quail hunt on the King Ranch. He invited me to accompany him. We didn't bring our hunting dogs because the handler on the ranch had his own dogs there. Milo and I talked about our love of watching the dogs work and the special relationship between a bird hunter and his dogs. I had bird dogs and took a lot of pride in them. That made hunting so much more enjoyable. Milo was the same way.

When our schedules allowed, he and I would go out for an evening meal on the road. We'd go to different places he liked. Pittsburgh was one of his favorite cities because of the fact he worked there and had relationships with so many people there.

I still see Milo often because we both continue to live in the Houston area and appear at various functions in the area. During the offseason, Milo is as active as anybody in baseball because he does so many different functions to raise money for charity or to honor people.

I often hear his broadcast of Hank Aaron breaking Babe Ruth's home run record. It's replayed so often. I actually saw it when it happened, but I was watching the Dodger broadcast because I was in Los Angeles at the time. I'm honored that Milo was able to call some of the highlights of my Houston career, including our postseason games in 1986.

Milo has a very special broadcast voice and presence on the air. When you hear the call of an event you were involved in and hear him call it, it makes it even more special to you because of his ability to express the moment over the air.

We're very fortunate to have this great Hall of Fame announcer in Houston.

During a major-league career that lasted 27 seasons, Nolan Ryan struck out 5,714 batters and hurled seven no-hitters—marks unlikely to fall. The native Texan owns a bank, two Astro farm clubs, and three cattle ranches, but still finds time to offer pitching instruction to Houston prospects. He and Milo were both with the Astros from 1985-88.

PREFACE

BY BILL GUILFOILE

The stories and anecdotes in the pages that follow reflect Milo Hamilton's knowledge of the game, his retentive memory, and an interest and enthusiasm that have made him a fan favorite in all five cities—Chicago, Pittsburgh, St. Louis, Atlanta, and Houston—where Milo has broadcast major league baseball. Milo Hamilton's listeners have the feeling they are actually in the ballpark with him, and that same sense is carried over in this book.

I can't imagine anyone overcoming a greater professional challenge than Milo did when he was hired by the Pirates as Bob Prince's successor in the broadcast booth at Three Rivers Stadium. As the Pittsburgh PR director at that time, I worked closely with the announcing team on a daily basis and was immediately impressed by Milo's attitude and approach as he started the 1976 season. He fully recognized that Prince had been a Pittsburgh institution for 28 years, with a signature style that had won him a huge following.

Soon, Milo's own personality and distinctive voice emerged, reflecting an integrity and skill that enabled him to develop and maintain a rapport and balance with athletes and management alike. Milo immediately proved himself a keen observer, a skilled reporter, and an accomplished broadcaster, culminating in his selection as the 1992 recipient of the prestigious Ford C. Frick Award, presented annually by the Baseball Hall of Fame for excellence in broadcasting.

Aware of my friendship with Milo, the Hall gave me the thrill of calling Milo and informing him of that honor. He joined an illustrious group of previous Frick awardees: Mel Allen, Red Barber, Bob Elson, Russ Hodges, Ernie Harwell, Vin Scully, Jack Brickhouse, Curt Gowdy, Buck Canel, Prince, Jack Buck, Lindsey Nelson, Harry Caray, By Saam, and Joe Garagiola. He's in good company.

I was tremendously impressed by Milo's acceptance speech during the 1992 Hall of Fame presentation ceremonies. His remarks were a thoughtful blend of seriousness and humor, of acknowledgement and appreciation, of reminiscence and personal experience. He spoke of his youth, growing up in Iowa, and of his teenage dream of becoming a sportscaster, of the adjustment required by a play-by-play announcer from doing a live broadcast one day and a game recreated from the Western Union ticker the next. He recalled the highlights of his life in the broadcast booth—especially the no-hitters and historic feats, including his memorable call of the Hank Aaron home run that broke Babe Ruth's career record. Milo expressed his thanks to the Chicago broadcasters who gave him opportunities and advice—Burt Wilson, Bob Elson, and Jack Brickhouse—and spoke of the managers, coaches, players, and front-office personnel who had a significant impact upon his career. Of course, he also remembered his parents, his wife, Arlene, and their children, Patricia and Mark, as well as personal friends who had made the trip to Cooperstown to share the occasion with him.

Especially important, aside from the speech's content, were the elegance and sincerity that permeated his remarks. Later in the day, I asked Milo if I could have a copy of his speech. It remains a significant artifact in the Hall of Fame library.

I hope that you find this book to be a significant artifact in your own library.

Bill Guilfoile spent 42 years in baseball public relations for the Yankees, Pirates, and the Baseball Hall of Fame. He was the 1966 recipient of the Robert O. Fishel Award for excellence in public relations. In retirement, he teaches public relations as an adjunct instructor on the faculty of Marian College in Fond du Lac, Wisconsin.

ACKNOWLEDGMENTS

This book would not have been possible without the support of Sports Publishing, especially acquisitions editor Bob Snodgrass and developmental editor Doug Hoepker.

A special thank you goes to Yvette Casares, advertising director of the Houston Astros, who provided a valuable e-mail link between the authors. Thanks also to Jimmy Stanton, media relations director of the Astros, for meeting several requests related to this project, and to my radio broadcast partner Alan Ashby, who put up with me before, during, and after this work was in progress.

I also appreciated the hospitality of Hotel Icon general manager Eric Adame, who provided luxurious working space in downtown Houston; Yvette Eichner of the Hyatt Penn's Landing in Philadelphia, where considerable interviewing was conducted; and the Glazier family, owners of The Strip House restaurant, for feeding the hungry authors while we were working.

I especially appreciate the ability of my longtime friend Bob Ibach, former public relations director of the Cubs, to recall my Chicago years so well and to recruit as lead writer Dan Schlossberg, who turned 400 single-spaced pages of interviews into a first-person narrative. Thanks also to photographer Stephen O'Brien, whose photograph adorns the cover of this book.

Nor could I have completed this project without the love, patience, and long-distance support of my grown children, Mark Hamilton and Patti Joy Watson, and their families.

And finally, thank you, thank you, thank you to the myriad of family, friends, and supporters who made the long and difficult trip to the funeral of my wife Arlene in February 2005, after spring training had started. To all of you who came, called, and wrote, and especially to Drayton McLane, Tim Purpura, Phil Garner, Nolan Ryan, my boss Jamie Hildreth, and past and present members of the

Houston Astros too numerous to detail here, I am forever appreciative.

—MILO HAMILTON
Houston, Texas
November 30, 2005

1

LIFE ON THE AIR

I t's plain and simple: baseball is a radio game. Fans use their imagination while listening to the broadcast to re-create the game. They're not locked into staring at a TV set for the better part of three hours. Baseball is a game a fan can take along for the ride. If there are errands to be run, you can listen to the game on the car radio. If there's work to be done in the yard or in the workshop, the radio keeps the game alive.

In my early years of broadcasting, it was my job to keep the game alive through re-creations. I would announce a game without actually being at the game, using wire service reports for information and sound effects to create the sound and feel of being at the ballpark. Those re-creations were popular; if people didn't want to hear baseball on the radio, would they have cared about hearing a re-created game? Not likely.

Through the response I get in person and via mail, I've learned that people often turn off the sound on the TV broadcast and turn on the radio announcer. That shows taste. Fans would rather hear the radio guy. That's why I really enjoy radio and have stuck with it all these years. I do radio by choice. I think the Astros were probably stunned eight or so years ago when I told them that I wanted to switch back to radio. It meant taking a sizeable salary cut, but I did it anyway. I like the latitude that radio presents, to be able to talk about the game in depth and weave in some stories. Storytelling in our game is important, and radio provides me with an ample opportunity to do just that.

I've been lucky to be on some real bell-ringer stations. Call it good fortune or just being in the right place at the right time, but by being on those top stations, I reached a lot of people over the years on my broadcasts. The Atlanta Braves had a big network when I was there in the late '60s and early '70s that reached far outside the state of Georgia, so I have a big following in Florida, Alabama, and the Carolinas. And people throughout Ohio, Pennsylvania, New York, and New Jersey know me from my time with KDKA—the flagship station for the Pittsburgh Pirates—in the late '70s. In St. Louis, the games were on KXOK when I was there in 1953-'54. They hadn't switched to KMOX yet. But there are still people who remember me from my days announcing Browns and Cardinals games. I was on WGN, a Chicago station with a powerful signal, when I worked for the Cubs. WCFL in Chicago had 50,000 watts of power and boasted a 100-station network in the early sixties. The station beamed east at night, so we had a lot of people in Indiana, Michigan, and Ohio listening in to our White Sox broadcast. And KTRH in Houston has a large broadcast range, too: we go way down in the valley near Corpus Christi and South Padre Island, and over into Louisiana and up into Arkansas and New Mexico.

Being a baseball announcer hasn't always been easy. As a broadcaster, I'm selling a product. I'm not selling tickets or a sponsor's goods, however; I'm selling baseball. But I can't be phony in my efforts. I can't say that a club is fabulous when it isn't. Luckily, I have never been told by anybody—a team owner or

Milo at his microphone in 1992, the year he entered the Baseball Hall of Fame.

otherwise—to take it easy in my analysis of a team. No one has ever asked me to be complimentary when a critical opinion was warranted.

The year that Drayton McLane bought the Astros, we headed to Colorado for a series with the Rockies. Doug Drabek—who had just been signed by Houston as a free agent—was enjoying a 7-0 lead in the game. But we blew that game in a miserable fashion. Drayton and his wife and two sons were on that trip, and the next morning, a Sunday, they came in to have breakfast in the coffee shop. I was there and Drayton came up to me and said, "Did you tell them about that game and how horrible it was?" I said "yes," and he responded, "Don't you ever change." Now if *that* wasn't carte blanche, I don't know what is.

Of course, there are some broadcasters who don't know when to let up on their criticism of a team or its players. We have to walk a line when being critical. If a player makes an error and it costs us the game, I have to address that mistake in my postgame wrap-up. If I don't, it's going to be in the beat writer's story the next day anyway. So if I don't tell people about the error that cost us the game, then they'll read the story the next day and wonder, "Why didn't Milo tell us how much that error hurt the club?" My credibility would become an issue for the listeners.

On the other side of the coin, it's imperative that the broadcaster takes the same approach as the ballplayer: we play every day, and every day is a new day. So the broadcaster cannot dwell on the mistakes of yesterday. Once that day is over, it's time to move on. I can't carry a grudge on to the next game. That can be difficult to do if the team is playing poorly.

Shortly after I came to Houston, Allen Russell, owner of the old Houston Buffs, and Clark Nealon, longtime *Houston Post* sports editor and a great baseball authority, told me, "If we were picking announcers for a club that wasn't very good, you'd be the first one. You're the best because you keep the interest up. You don't ever let it sound like the club isn't in contention." Over my career, I've been with plenty of clubs that weren't very good, and my approach has always been that of an optimist. My theory is this: I owe it to the fan, to the ballclub, and to the sponsors, who spend a lot of dollars, to maintain a positive attitude about the team.

If you know anything about my style, enthusiasm and spontaneity have always been my long suit. A losing team is not an excuse to lose interest. Don't forget: when I came to Houston, former Astros owner John McMullen had decided to rebuild the club. That opened the door for the Caminitis and the Biggios to come along and form the basis of what became a pretty good club. In 1991, when Art Howe was managing, it looked like we might lose 100 games. Still, I felt that I owed it to all those people to keep the broadcast fair. The real fan may be discouraged because the team is losing, but that fan still wants to listen to the games. My job, my obligation, and my duty is to make that broadcast a great broadcast.

Judging by the response I've received from the teams I've covered, I must have done a pretty good job. Players and managers might disagree with something that I've said, but they are rarely upset to the point where it becomes a distraction or an argument. In my career, only one player and a couple of managers have complained about my broadcast.

The player was Carl Morton, who pitched for the Braves. If Carl was ahead in the fifth or sixth inning, he'd start looking to the bullpen for help. He felt he had done his job, and he was ready to leave the game and earn a victory. I like the type of pitcher who stays in there until he's out of gas or the manager comes to get him, not someone who keeps looking like he wants out of the game. The knock on Carl was that he was always looking to get out of a game with a lead. During one game, Carl began to get antsy and peer toward the dugout. On the broadcast I said, "I'd like to see Carl Morton finish some more games, because he's got a track record of not finishing."

Well, he got home that night and a neighbor told him what I said. He asked me about it the next day and I said, "Okay, Carl, let me ask you a question: How long have I been doing games with you?" He said, "Two or three years." Carl's wife used to tell me how she liked the way I talked about Carl on the air—how he was talented and a good pitcher. I knew that his family listened to the games and was aware of all of my previous comments about Carl. So I said, "Carl, I don't remember you ever coming to me and thanking me for all of the good things I said about you. So I'm not thrilled about you asking me about this one time." And that was the end of our conversation.

I also had a problem with Bobby Bragan, who managed the Braves in Milwaukee and then came with the team to Atlanta. He thought my broadcast partner, Ernie Johnson, and I were second-guessing him on the air. The club was bad, and some of the decisions he was making leant themselves to discussion. For instance, Bragan tried to convert outfielder Rico Carty into a catcher, and then he benched lefthanded slugger Eddie Mathews against lefthanded pitchers near the end of his career.

Bragan was fired two-thirds of the way through the 1966 season and replaced by Billy Hitchcock. The night Hitchcock took over, the Braves were playing the Dodgers. Denny Lemaster was to pitch for the Braves against lefty Sandy Koufax. Even with a tough lefthander pitching, Hitchcock wrote Mathews's name on the lineup card. A sell-out crowd of 53,000 waited through rain delays as the game carried on past midnight. Koufax was still pitching late in the game, but Lemaster had departed, despite pitching a hell of a game. Unfortunately, we didn't score any runs for him. Then in the wee hours of the morning, Mathews hit a home run off Koufax to win the game. Hitchcock put Mathews back in the lineup against the lefty even though Bragan had thought Mathews was at the end of the trail. And we talked about that on the air, much to Bragan's disgust.

To his credit, Bragan is a great guy and a wonderful storyteller—one of baseball's greatest salesmen. I've seen Bragan many times over the years, and he's never once said boo after that initial reaction. I think he was just frustrated at his situation. He was from Birmingham, Alabama, and was disappointed that he couldn't win in front of his "home" folks in the South.

In addition to being honest, I also learned early on to never socialize with the players. I will never forget what somebody once said to me while I was broadcasting for the old Three-I League at Davenport, Iowa, in the early '50s: "We think you're going to be a big-league announcer some day, but I just want to give you a bit of advice. Don't ever socialize with the players in your capacity as a broadcaster. If anything goes awry or there's something of a scandal, the ballclub will always stick up for the player, but they'll never stick up for you." I took that advice to heart. Other broadcasters have mixed with the players, and it certainly got them into some deep trouble. I don't leave anything to chance.

As a broadcaster, I don't want to know if a certain player spent the previous night out on the town. Maybe the next day the player goes 0-for-5 at the plate or gets knocked out in the second inning. I don't want that knowledge in the back of my mind—that I saw a player out late having fun—because then I might deduce that his actions off the field were the reason he didn't play well on the field.

If I don't know about it, then I'm better off. After all, I'm not a scandal reporter or a gossip columnist. So that sort of detail never makes it into my broadcasts.

Accuracy is a big deal for me as well when it comes to my analysis of the game. If a game is tied in the eighth inning, I might reference a missed scoring opportunity we had earlier in the game. If I neglect to bring that point up, I'm not doing my job as a reporter. I want my listeners to hear the whole story—even if that means giving credit to the other team when they make a spectacular play or a wise decision. I might praise another team's outfielder if he hits a home run or makes a great diving catch. Some fans may not like that I spend time talking about the opposition, but keep in mind that I may not have seen that player in action for a month or more, and I might not see him again for another month. So, the opportunities to discuss his talent and performance are few and far between.

I make certain to report the score frequently, too, in case the listener was away from the radio for a bit and is checking back in. Red Barber, the longtime voice of the Brooklyn Dodgers, had a little egg timer on his desk. When it ran out, he gave the score. I just let common sense dictate when it's time to mention which team is winning.

I don't openly root for my ballclub—I'm not what one would call a "homer"—but that doesn't mean that I don't do everything in my power to make sure they win. Like ballplayers, I have little superstitions that I adhere to in order to help the team win. For example, I do a pregame show every day with the manager. If we won the night before, I make the manager sit in the same chair and I sit in the same chair. If we lost, we change chairs. In addition, I fill out my lineup card a certain way based on whether we won or lost the previous game. Everyone has their own superstitions or quirks. Some of them just make more sense than others.

2

FIELD OF DREAMS

'm a Depression kid. I grew up in the farm belt, in Iowa, during the 1930s. It wasn't easy living: we went through the stock market crash, the Dust Bowl, and plagues of crop-eating bugs. My paternal great-grandfather came from County Tyrone in northern Ireland. He lived until I was about four or five years old, and I remember his speaking voice because of his distinctive brogue.

My dad's first name is Milo. But I didn't know the origins of the name until after my dad passed away when I was 34 years old. My dad's older sister, Mabel, told me my dad was born in 1903, when the Iowa Secretary of Agriculture was Milo Reno. My grandma liked the name and decided to name her son after Milo Reno. My full name is Leland Milo Hamilton. But nobody ever called me Leland after I was 10 years old except for my mother. When my dad passed away, she gave up and switched to Milo like everyone else. Between the fourth and the fifth grade, all the guys in my neighborhood decided to call each other by our middle names. When we went back to school, the gag stopped—except for me. I was known as L. Milo when I was growing up. I never used the initial. But they did it to differentiate between my dad and me.

When I was born in 1927, my dad was earning $12 a week working for a firm that sold coal and feed for cattle and hogs. After the stock market crash two years later, he went to work for a coal and shipping association and was named a manager. He never went to high school, but did attend a business college, which a lot of people did back in the teens and twenties.

By the mid-'30s, he was all the way up to $25 a week, right in the midst of the Great Depression. He was glad to have a job, but I remember he had to go to work at six in the morning and he worked till six at night. I remember he took a long nap on Sunday because it was a tough life.

When I was in the eighth grade, my dad and another fellow bought a grain elevator. That was very hazardous because the elevator served as a natural flue. When fire destroyed it, he had a brand new truck and a lot of feed that he hadn't yet paid for. His pride wouldn't let him declare bankruptcy, so he went to work at the Iowa Ordnance Plant from 6 a.m. to 6 p.m., six days a week. That's 72 hours a week. By doing all that hard work and then dying at the age of 57, I often wonder if my dad did the right thing. Instead of going bankrupt—which wasn't dishonest—he paid off all his debts and it took a terrible toll on him. My mother also worked for the county auditor and stayed there until a few years before she passed away. It became a full-time job and helped to pay off those debts.

Iowa—like several other surrounding states—went through a horrible drought in the mid-'30s—the Dust Bowl. On some days it was nearly impossible to see, and it destroyed my dad's garden because there was no rain. A lot of farmers went under. My grandfather, a landowner all of his life, lost his farm. He rented farms after that but never really recovered.

Besides the dust, there was a problem with the chinch bug, which ate the crops on my grandfather's farm. I could hear the

Milo at age seven in 1933, with his parents, Cleo and Milo.

noise they made as they were devouring a cornfield. The bugs were destroying everything the drought hadn't already doomed. Those were tough years. A lot of people lost everything. Even wealthy people in my little town of Fairfield never recovered. We managed somehow. We sold what vegetables my dad's garden did produce, and we ate food that we grew. Once in a while, my grandfather would slaughter a hog or a cow and give us some of that. My mother shopped every Saturday night after we went to the movie, and she never spent more than $3. That was the grocery bill for the week.

Some people didn't have a dollar to their name. There were a lot of hobos around. Whenever a hobo rang at the back door, my mother gave him an apple or a peanut butter sandwich. She never turned anyone away. But she didn't want to make them think they got something for nothing, so she'd make them do a little chore, like raking the yard. News of her kindness spread, too: the hobos always left something on a bush in our yard, as a signal to other hobos that they could get something at our house.

Things weren't all bad for me as a kid, though. I played coronet in the band, sang in all of the musical groups, and always had the lead in the school plays. Times were tight, but my mom always found a quarter to pay for my singing lessons. She encouraged my singing, not only for the experience, but because it was enjoyable. She knew I got a kick out of being in front of a crowd. My mom was also active in the church, so I always sang in the choir and at recitals.

At that time, my dad was a bigwig in the masonic lodge, a fraternal organization that was popular in a lot of small towns. Through his ties with the lodge, my dad was always performing and speaking at masonic gatherings around southeast Iowa. I must have gotten some of my speaking ability from him. I never realized it because I never saw him in front of people. But some of that had to be in my genes.

I had to give up the coronet in the fall of my junior year because I wasn't a very good student and had too many extracurricular activities. Three mornings a week, I had to be at band practice at 7:30. Two other mornings, I had mixed chorus practice. That fall we did *Here Comes Mr. Jordan*, a play where the lead never leaves the stage. I had to memorize 500 lines for that play, and the time commitment took its toll. The chemistry teacher finally went to the high school principal and said, "You need to have a talk with Milo, because there's no way I can pass him." I was barely passing any class at the time. So I decided to quit the band.

Unfortunately for me, the bandmaster was very possessive of the people he instructed. If a band member quit band, he turned on that person like a viper. It happened to me, as well as two of my friends. Right before the basketball season was going to start in my junior year, the band director told Turk Balderson, the football and basketball coach, "You shouldn't have anything to do with Milo. He's a no-good person who quits everything." To his credit, Turk didn't listen to the advice. Instead, he judged me for what I was. In high school, a player had to furnish his own shoes until he made the varsity squad. Turk came along, threw the shoes down at my feet, and said, "Go get a locker with the varsity."

The way I was failing subjects, I'm glad Turk didn't give up on me. It was great to know that somebody cared. And later that basketball season, I had to miss a Friday night basketball game. I had qualified for the statewide declamatory contest in the humorous division, doing a bit from the film *Green Pastures*. This was January of 1944, and I was the first Fairfield High School student to make the state finals in a declamatory contest in 30 years. I went in to talk to Turk about missing the game because I felt he should be the one to make the call. He said, "You're going to play in a lot more games, but you need to go to that speech contest." Turk felt it was important for me to attend and represent the school. He was a guy who really influenced my life.

As for my playing skills, the real reason I made the basketball team was because they had to have 12 guys. That's also the reason I made the football team; they needed 48 guys. We didn't have a baseball team, but I played hardball in the old country league. Softball was the big game in the '30s, and we played from morning 'til night. With no high school baseball team, my introduction to baseball came through that league.

All the small towns with country schools had teams. My uncle played on the team, and my dad was kind of a participating manager. We played in a cow pasture on the Stoner Farm north of Fairfield. That's where I saw my first live baseball. When the war broke out and some of the older guys had to serve overseas, I became the team's shortstop at the age of 14. I couldn't hit a lick, but I could sure play some shortstop.

We took up a collection so we could pay for bats and balls. A player could also send away for a set of spikes—the actual metal spikes—and then have a shoe cobbler rivet them on to an old pair of shoes. That's how I got my first pair of spikes when I was 10 years old.

At the games, there would be a great big washtub filled with ice, which would cool the Coca Cola (it came in those old green bottles), frosty orange drinks, strawberry drinks, and creme sodas. The women would bring food, and it was kind of like an early version of tailgating. There was a game or two every weekend, and it was our entertainment. It didn't cost anything.

Growing up in Iowa in the 1930s, I remember everyone talking about Bob Feller. His dad caught him out in the barn in the winter so he could throw. And before he got his high school diploma, he pitched in a big-league game and struck out 17. He was a high school kid from Van Meter, Iowa, and we were all ga-ga over him.

My hometown was Fairfield, population 7,000, or just under half that of the county. Fairfield was located in the southeast corner of the state, and the nearest big city—Des Moines, Iowa—was 120 miles away. My high school was in the Little Six Conference with Washington, Burlington, Fort Madison, Muscatine, Ottumwa, and Mount Pleasant. When I was in the seventh and eighth grades, Fairfield High School won the conference in football. My dad always took me to the high school games on Friday night and to Parsons College games on Saturday afternoon. So I had fandom pounded into me at an early age because my dad was a big fan.

We all listened to WHO, a 50,000-watt station from Des Moines, for the news and other programs. It featured a lot of live music in those days as well; they weren't playing records yet on the radio. This was in the mid-'30s, and Ronald "Dutch" Reagan was the sports announcer. He did the Iowa football games, and he re-created Cubs games. One legendary story about Reagan's re-creation days recalls him announcing a game with a long rain delay—when there was no rain delay. The Western Union ticker had broken down, and so Reagan chose to fill the space by inserting a rain delay. Reagan also had a sports show every night at 10:15, after the news at 10 with H.R. Gross, who later became a U.S. Congressman from Iowa. My mom said I could stay up to listen to Dutch Reagan, but at 10:30 I had to be in bed.

I met Reagan several years later when he was president and had come home to California for a respite. He and Nancy were at Dodger Stadium, and I asked Dodgers general manager Fred Claire if I could meet him. He arranged it with the Secret Service and I went down to those seats right behind the screen at Dodger Stadium, the low seats that are the worst seats in the park. I met him, told him who I was, and then took him for a walk down memory lane. When he signed off every night, Reagan had to deliver an advertising message from his show's sponsor, Kentucky Club Pipe Tobacco: "Be sure to look for the blue pack with a red-coated rider." All those years later, I delivered the same line to him. He said, "How'd you remember that?" I replied, "Because I heard you every night as a kid growing up back in Iowa." He liked that.

I remember Reagan being a good broadcaster. I recall him broadcasting an Iowa football game when they were playing UCLA on the coast and an Iowa back was running for a touchdown. As the running back neared the goal line, he fumbled the ball. Reagan's call of the play was, "He *blankety-blank* dropped the ball." Of course, using an expletive wasn't acceptable. It might not have cost him his job, but it might have caused him to look for employment elsewhere. While he was out in Los Angeles, some of his friends in the movie industry got him a screen audition, and that's how he eventually became a movie star.

Years later, I was hoping to do the same thing. Maurice Seymour was the photographer of the stars, both film and recording artists. He had studios in L.A. and Chicago, and a friend of mine suggested that I have Seymour take some portraits of me. He had me pose as if I were a movie star, watching the way I folded

Milo poses for a portrait by Maurice Seymour, photographer of the stars. Hollywood never called. © 1978 Maurice Seymour/MPTV.net

my arms or had my chin on my hands. The pictures were great considering the subject, but Hollywood never called.

I had grown up watching Clark Gable, Jimmy Stewart, Douglas Fairbanks, all those famous actors. In the '30s, when you went to the movies on a Saturday night, there was a promotion called Bank Night at a lot of the small-town theaters in which they gave away money. My folks often went along with me. The admission was 11 cents for kids and 36 cents for adults. We would go on a Saturday afternoon and watch the serials: *Tom Mix, The Green Hornet, Buck Rogers*. And I could stay all day in the theater for 11 cents and just keep watching them. Then on Saturday night, I went to the movie with my folks.

There was no television in those days, just radio. Everyone listened to the ballgames. I listened to Bob Elson do Cubs games when I could get WGN tuned in. I remember Bob Elson's sponsors in the mid-'30s: Old Gold cigarettes, Walgreen's drugstore and, on the weekends, Tutti-Fruiti ice cream. When I met Elson years later, I gave him one of the lines from his commercials just as I had done with Reagan. He was quite impressed that this little kid from Iowa remembered his broadcast, whom he was broadcasting for, and who the sponsors were.

I grew up rooting for the St. Louis Cardinals. I didn't have much say in the matter because my dad was the biggest Cardinal fan in Fairfield, Iowa. We stuck out because in those days you were either a Cubs or White Sox fan. It was easy to get on the train and go into Chicago and see a game. But my dad rooted for the Cardinals.

In 1938, the year after Ducky Medwick won the Triple Crown, *The Baseball Register* had Medwick's picture on the cover. I wanted to buy a copy, but it was an expensive 15 cents. Bread in those days cost six cents, but if you waited till the next day, the bakery would sell its day-old bread for a nickel. My mom often gave me the penny difference. Sometimes I would buy a stick of licorice or a jawbreaker—or I would just save the penny. I saved 15 pennies to buy that *Baseball Register* from the cigar store. In those days, all the cigar stores had a ticker and a blackboard in the window where they wrote the ball scores. I'd go by the store after school and see what the ball scores were from that day.

I was upset when The Cardinals traded Medwick to the Brooklyn Dodgers. At dinner one night, I announced that I was now a Dodgers fan. My dad said, "Oh, I don't think so. You can be a Ducky Medwick fan as long as you want to be, but you're always a Cardinals fan."

Well, dad was sort of right: I remained a *baseball* fan for sure.

3

A LUCKY BREAK

I was a freshman when the United States entered World War II at the end of 1941. It happened on a Sunday. I was in a high school that had about 500 students, and on Monday, the principal said, "We're at war." World War I was fresh in our minds, because some of our parents had been involved. My dad missed it because he was a teenager when World War I came, but a lot of his friends and a lot of the people in my little town fought in it.

In my senior year, the war was still going on. While it was about ready to end in Europe, it was ongoing in Japan. After our high school basketball season ended in February, five of us went down to the recruiting station in the post office and joined the Navy. About a month later, the recruiting station called a couple of us, but we weren't finished with school yet. Our high school principal went down there and told the recruiters, "You've got to let these two kids get their high school diplomas." By golly, they went for

it. We crossed the stage for graduation in mid-May, and only days later I was at Great Lakes Naval Air Station. I was never in combat, though. I was in a convoy going to Japan in case there was going to be an invasion, but when the atomic bombs dropped, no invasion was necessary.

I still can't believe how my broadcasting career got started. It was really a fluke. As a young Navy Seabee at the end of the war, my outfit was sent to Guam. I opened up the *Navy News* one morning and on the front of the paper was a picture of three attractive girls—guaranteed to catch the eye of servicemen overseas. They were a part of the USO called "civilian actress technicians." Their mission in Guam was to put on a Broadway play and tour the island for 30 days (there were 30 outdoor theaters on the island at the time).

The play they chose was *My Sister Eileen*, about a young girl who went to New York, her sister, and a drugstore manager. They were holding auditions that night at the 20th Air Force Base and I said, "You know, I've been in all those plays in high school. What the heck?" So I went up there, auditioned, and got the part of the young drugstore manager. Three guys from Armed Forces Radio on Guam were also there. Two of them got parts and the other was named the stage manager.

The program director of the Navy's radio station on Guam, who happened to be one of those three guys, told me one of the older guys was going to be discharged and they were looking for an announcer. He asked me if I'd ever been on the air. I replied "No," but told them that in my little hometown of Fairfield, Iowa, my church group used to go about 20 miles to a little radio station in Ottumwa, where we'd put on programs with the choir. I had done a lot of singing as a youngster, but I'd never been on the air. The Navy radio guys liked my voice, so I auditioned for them the next weekend and was offered a job. They arranged the paperwork and told me to come at 2:30 p.m. because I was going on the air at 3 p.m. The guy who was leaving was supposed to show me all the ropes.

Guam is in the Pacific, part of the chain of islands known as the Marianas. The radio station was in Admiral Nimitz' fleet

Milo behind his first microphone while serving in the U.S. Navy in Guam. This was taken three months after his 18th birthday in 1945.

headquarters, a big Quonset hut that was the only air-conditioned building in the Pacific. The exec of the radio station was a young Marine lieutenant who might have been 21 years old. A Navy commander was the head of the station, but the Marine lieutenant was handling everything. At 2:45 p.m.—15 minutes before I was due to start my first shift—the lieutenant did the station break and told me to pay attention. He didn't write down anything but said into the mike, "This is WXLI, the voice of Guam, serving the Marianas high atop Mt. Agana. The time is 2:45."

Over the next several minutes, I memorized the phrase, saying it over and over. At three o'clock, the red light came on and I was on the air. The first words out of my mouth: "This is WXLI, the voice of Guam, serving the Marianas high atop Mt. Agana, from Fleet Admiral Nimitz' headquarters, with air-conditioned studios. The time is 2:45." The only problem was that it was 3 o'clock. I had memorized the phrase, but I forgot to update the time. When I went into the Baseball Hall of Fame in 1992, I told the crowd, "Can you imagine a guy who went on the air the first time and couldn't even give the correct time is now going into the Hall of Fame?"

I really fell in love with broadcasting. But I was a kid who had just turned 18 and didn't know what I wanted to do with my life. My dad didn't have any business that I was going to go into. I probably wasn't going to go to college, unless I got some financial help from somewhere or someone. Then, a specific path was laid out before me that started my course to where I am today. A few weeks after my less-than-stellar debut on the air, the station manager announced that the Pacific baseball tournament was coming to Guam and suggested that we broadcast some of those games. He wanted to know if anybody had ever announced a game. "No," I said, summoning up some courage, "but I've listened to a lot of games and played country hardball." He replied, "You're it."

I tried to remember everything I'd heard Bob Elson say on WGN radio when I was a kid. I did the baseball games and thought to myself, "Boy, I think this is what I want to do." When I came back from the Navy, I did go to college. There was a small Presbyterian school in my hometown named Parsons College. We had about 500 students, twice the usual amount for the school as there were a lot of veterans returning from the war and entering college. I stayed there for two years, and worked on a radio station at the college and a station in nearby Ottumwa. The latter—KBIZ—was the same station that I had sung on as a kid.

The speech teacher at Parsons College, who was also the drama director, had graduated from the University of Iowa. She told me, "I think you need to go to Iowa rather than stay here and finish at Parsons. They've got a full-time radio station. I think it would really enhance your career." She was right. The University of Iowa had an AM and an FM station, and students were the broadcasters

Milo interviews famous bandleader Duke Ellington in 1948 for WSUI, the University of Iowa radio station.

and were responsible for everything. It was a great station with a lot of history. I had a chance to spin some records there in addition to being a sports broadcaster.

Since I had transferred there as a junior, I was low on the totem pole of the station's sports staff. So I wrote copy instead of broadcasting. Then during my senior year, I was on some sports shows. During the summers, I took a trolley to nearby Cedar Rapids, Iowa, and broadcast dance remotes at the spacious Archer Ballroom. I did Lawrence Welk when he led a little six-piece territory band. I also did The Dorsey Brothers Orchestra, Benny Goodman, and Charlie Spivak, who at the time was known as "the sweetest trumpet this side of Heaven."

I earned $7.50 for each of those remotes, and that's how I bought my meal tickets to eat in the restaurant in Iowa City. For the shows I was doing on the University station, I was earning 80 cents per show. So I was getting $4 a week. Hey, it was better than a kick in the shins. The GI bill was paying my tuition, but I needed that meal money.

In my senior year, broadcaster Bob Brooks—who worked the Iowa Hawkeyes football and basketball games for over 50 years— took a liking to me and used me as his sidekick. I didn't get paid, but I didn't care. Our last football game that year was at Notre Dame. I was going to go home and he was going to go to Florida for a few days. As we were walking to the car, he handed me a box of ROI-TAN cigars—they were only a nickel at that time— because I smoked cigars once in a while. That was my "pay" for the Iowa football season that year. When he returned, I worked basketball games with him. It was an honor to be able to put on my resume when I graduated that I had done games with Bob Brooks.

As I readied myself for graduation, I went home to Fairfield for the Christmas holidays. I visited a friend of my dad's who knew the sales manager and part-owner of a radio station in the Quad Cities, which were Davenport, Iowa, and three towns across the river in Illinois: Moline, East Moline, and Rock Island. He contacted the sales manager, G. Lavern Flambo, and told him that I was going to be graduating from college soon and was looking for work. Flambo

used to attend church with my family and had sung in the choir
with me, and was interested in meeting me. He came to see me and
asked, "Could you get on the train in the next few days and come
to Moline so we can audition you?" A few weeks before, I had
broadcast a fictitious Cardinals baseball game and saved it onto a
great big disk to use as a sample while looking for work. The
station listened to the sample and hired me.

When I graduated five weeks later in February of 1950, I went
home from school with my folks on a Saturday, then left for
Moline the next day, and went to work the following day.

4

A CAREER BEGINS

My first day on the job at WQUA, I had to do 16 Golden Globe fights. I had never been to a boxing match or even seen one. But I had heard Clem McCarthy do the Joe Louis fights, because my dad and I used to listen to them on his old, staticy Atwater Kent radio. The start of the fights was delayed for a good while because so much snow had fallen on Sunday and Monday, making it difficult for people to get there on time. G. Lavern Flambo was there and decided that the broadcast would go on in spite of the weather. So, we interviewed the boxing referee and some of the trainers, too, to fill time. I did alright calling one match, even though I'm sure I called certain punches by the wrong names. By 11 o'clock that night, I knew I had the broadcast bug. It was my first actual day of work at my first real job—just 48 hours after I graduated from Iowa—and I was excited. I was earning $42.50 a week and working 60 hours per week.

I was soon given the opportunity to announce high school basketball games. I did 30 games the first month I was out of school, followed by the Iowa boys high school tournament, which included 16 games in five days. I enjoyed broadcasting basketball games, but one of the main reasons that I took the job in Moline was to broadcast Three-I League baseball games. The Quad City Tigers, located in Davenport, were a Detroit Tigers farm team.

Broadcasting baseball games in those days—especially road games—was a completely different experience from what I'm accustomed to now. We traveled for a few road games, but mostly we re-created away games with information from the teletype. If I was doing a Quad City Tigers game at a Davenport station but the team was playing in Terre Haute, Indiana, we'd do the game without ever seeing it. A guy at the away ballpark, usually a moonlighting railroad telegrapher, would be dot-dashing to another railroad guy who was moonlighting at my studio in Davenport. That's how I received the information that I then re-created on air.

When Dan Carnavelli, the player-manager for Terre Haute, was batting, the telegraph guy would hand me the sheet: Dan Carnavelli, B-1 [ball one]; Next pitch, B-2 [ball two]; Then S-1S [strike one, swinging]; S-2C [strike two, called]; Single to left. I had to fill in all the gaps by improvising: "Into the wind-up, here's the pitch, there's a curve ball, and he swings and misses."

I recall one re-creation of a double-header between the Quad City Tigers and the Decatur Cubs. One of the games went 17 innings, and there were 37 walks in the double-header. In this particular instance, I already knew the outcome of the game before I re-created it. So I skipped pitches to get the ball in play a little sooner, otherwise we would have been there all night.

I re-created some basketball games as well. During my first month on the air, I re-created some of the Quad City Black Hawks basketball games. That team is now the Atlanta Hawks. At the time, Ben Kerner was the owner, and the legendary Red Auerbach was the coach. The Black Hawks were the dominant team in their league so we re-created their basketball games in the afternoon. We had a guy in the studio who blew a whistle to indicate a foul or

Milo's first job after college: sports director of WQUA in Moline, Illinois.

time-out if given a signal from the announcer. And we also had crowd noise. After the basketball game was over, I'd then broadcast a baseball game in the evening.

I credit those re-creations with getting me to the big leagues sooner. It helped me learn all the players, including the pitchers and what they threw, so I became somewhat knowledgeable about the game. If a guy like little Jack Meyer, a pitcher for the Phillies, was in the game, I had a pretty good idea that he was throwing some sliders. I might not have been accurate in guessing what pitch was thrown, but it sounded like a ball game to the listener. The additional sound effects helped out, too. We went out to the ballpark early in the season and recorded the crowd's reaction to singles, doubles, triples, and home runs. We also sampled the vendors and the PA announcer. So to the listener, our broadcasts felt genuine. In fact, Marv Owen, who got thrown out of the World Series along with Ducky Medwick in the 1930s, was the Quad Cities manager at that time. Our studios were in the Davenport hotel, where he and his wife lived that summer. Marv's wife was so enamored with the way the radio station made the game sound real that she used to come to the station and watch me broadcast live.

We had to have a team effort at the station when we were doing the minor league re-creations. The guy running the board, who would have been playing records normally, put a wastepaper basket over his head to make himself sound like the PA man giving the starting lineups at the ballpark. Then he played the National Anthem into an echo chamber to make it sound like it was being played at the ballpark. As the Western Union sheet came across reading SINGLE TO RIGHT, I'd say, "And there's a single to right field" as the crowd reaction to a "single" would air.

As late as 1965, we were still re-creating games in the afternoons on the White Sox network, usually between other American League clubs. Chicago's 1961 season ended on a Saturday night in Baltimore with a 4-3 loss. The season was supposed to end the following day; instead, it wrapped up a day early by mutual agreement between the two clubs, because Johnny Unitas and the Baltimore Colts needed the stadium for a football game on Sunday. Well, the station was still obligated to broadcast a game on the final day of the season, and we decided to re-create the Yankees-Red Sox game. It turned out to be the game in which Roger Maris hit his 61st home run to break Babe Ruth's record for a season. It was the only run either team scored in the game.

In those days, the White Sox studios were located at the old Furniture Mart on Lake Shore Drive. I got on the elevator the day after broadcasting Maris's legendary game, and some of the people

Milo is honored for working 100 basketball games in a single season while at KSTT in Davenport, Iowa.

who worked for the furniture store were coming in to work. A few of them asked me, "How in the world did you get back here so fast? I heard you do the Maris game yesterday from Yankee Stadium." They had no idea that I was re-creating the game from a ticker.

My station was sold in the middle of the football season that fall and the new owners announced that they weren't going to be a sports station anymore. I moved across the river to KSTT in Davenport, Iowa, and told the station manager, "There's going to be a void in this market. Somebody needs to be doing these games." It was a market of about 250,000 people, with four high schools and two colleges. When the owner said, "I've never done sports on my station," I suggested a trial run. We did five football games that first weekend I was at that station. The owner received a positive reaction and said, "I think you've sold me on this thing." I drew up an ambitious schedule of 50 basketball games plus the state tournament.

The Davenport baseball team followed me to KSTT. But after the 1952 season, the team was planning to move to Peoria, Illinois. I didn't know what my future was at the station, and I was embroiled in a big basketball schedule again. It just happened that the Chicago White Sox were looking for a sidekick for their long-time announcer, Bob Elson. He'd never had a partner, because all the old guys worked alone. I knew Bill Rigney, an executive who was the general manager of the Waterloo team in the Three-I League, a White Sox farm team. He and his brother John Rigney, who was married to Dorothy Comiskey, used to come to some of the minor-league games. So I sent him a tape and he gave it to his radio station, WCFL, "the voice of labor in Chicago." It was a 50,000-watt station that carried the White Sox games.

The application and interview process went on all winter. It came down to me and Don Wells, who got the job. He deserved it, as he was older and he had done games for Gordon McClendon, the old Scotsman, on the Liberty Network. He had a nice career with Elson and was later one of the original broadcasters when the Los Angeles Angels became a franchise in 1961.

I didn't realize it at the time, but I would get an opportunity to work with Elson just a few years later. In the meantime, I needed to find a job for 1953 and was hoping it might be in the major leagues.

5

ST. LOUIS BLUES

At KSTT in Davenport, Iowa, our broadcasts were financially aided by the "KSTT Sports Caravan." We sold 20 commercials per game to various sponsors, from auto dealers to appliance and furniture stores. One of our sponsors was Hanson Sporting Goods store, managed by Don Lynch. Two people from Rawlings Sporting Goods, Elmer Blasco and Kenny Baldwin, were coming to town to show Don their new lines, since he sold football equipment to all the local high schools. Don asked me to come down and maybe do a tape with Rawlings and use it on my show, and I agreed.

The representatives from Rawlings liked the show so much that they asked Don if they could get a tape. I got them a tape and they went back to St. Louis, where they were building a new TV station that was going on the air in the spring. They already had a deal in place to be the television station for the St. Louis Browns. They took my tape to the program director, Ted Westcott. He called me up and hired me over the phone to be his television guy and work on the Browns games. He said, "Now come to St. Louis and let's get this contract signed."

When I walked into his office, I said, "What would you have done if I'd have walked in here and looked like Boris Karloff in *Frankenstein*?" He said the guys from Rawlings told him that I wasn't a bad-looking guy. He also said he loved my voice and my enthusiasm. So I did the six o'clock and 10 o'clock sports for KTVI-TV in St. Louis. And I was on the Browns' staff—finally broadcasting in the major leagues.

The Browns were a bad ball club that didn't draw well at the gate. Some nights we had more ushers than fans. Bill Veeck, who had previously enjoyed so much success as owner of the Cleveland Indians, had tried all kinds of memorable ploys to bring people to the ballpark. Veeck is most remembered for allowing Eddie Gaedel, a midget, to pop out of a cake and then stride to the plate to bat in a game. But he also asked fans to make strategy decisions for the team on "Grandstand Managers Day." And he recruited legendary Negro League hurler Satchel Paige to pitch for both the Indians and the Browns.

But most of that happened before I arrived. By 1953, it was a foregone conclusion that the club was going to relocate. We had some decent ball players. Don Larsen, Bob Turley, and Paige were the best pitchers, but we also featured some good position players in Vern Stephens, Billy Hunter, Roy Sievers, Hank Edwards, Vic Wertz, and Clint "Scrap Iron" Courtney. But overall our team wasn't very good.

Larsen was never a great guy for discipline. He broke team curfew all the time. In one game against the Indians, Larsen was struggling. Early Wynn, who was pitching for Cleveland, got three or four doubles against him. But Marty Marion, manager of the Browns, was determined to teach Larsen a lesson. "I'm going to show this big guy that I'm the manager," he said. So he left Larsen in for the whole game even though the score was 18-2. But his message still didn't sink in.

Milo's big league career began in 1953 with the St. Louis Browns. He's featured here in an advertisement for WTVI along with other Browns announcers, including Dizzy Dean.

Larsen and Turley later moved to Baltimore with the team but were soon traded to the Yankees in the famous 17-player deal, the biggest trade of all time. Paul Richards engineered the trade because he wanted little Willie Miranda, a terrific fielder, to play shortstop for the Orioles. In the meantime, somebody had the good sense to make Turley and Larsen pitch out of the stretch— like there was somebody on base—all of the time. It must have been Jim Turner, the pitching coach of the Yankees then. The no-windup deliveries changed both of their careers: Larsen pitched a perfect game in the World Series in 1956 and Turley won a Cy Young in 1958.

I was low man on the totem pole when I started with the '53 Browns. Buddy Blattner and Dizzy Dean, the two main commentators for the Browns, went away on weekends to do the Game of the Week for Falstaff Beer, so I got a chance to fill in. I was doing mostly pregame and postgame on TV for the Browns, and then filling in on radio when Blattner and Dean went out of town.

When the Browns moved to Baltimore after that season, the team had its own people in mind. Ernie Harwell went over there, and Bob Murphy came a year later. So I was out of work once again. I had been doing St. Louis University basketball that winter for Anheuser-Busch. When the brewery bought the Cardinals, it wanted somebody to work with Harry Caray, who was closely associated with Griesedieck Beer. With my Anheuser-Busch background, I was the logical guy. So, I stuck around St. Louis and joined the Cardinals broadcast team.

In 1954, I traveled with Caray during the first half of the season, and then Jack Buck, who had been the AAA announcer at Rochester, traveled with Caray during the second half. At the All-Star break, Buck went on the road and I stayed back at the TV station and did the pre- and post-game in the studio. And I did the radio sports shows on the station, which was KOKX in St. Louis.

The 1954 season was memorable for me because I saw Hank Aaron hit his first home run, as an opposing player. I saw Wally Moon, who replaced Enos Slaughter with the Cardinals, become

Rookie of the Year. And I got the chance to be around manager Eddie Stanky for a year.

I first met Stanky on our initial road trip of the season. I hadn't been to spring training, so Stanky didn't know me from a fence post. After one game in which Gerry Staley had just lost a tough, close decision, beat writer Bob Broeg said to me, "Wait here or go up by the clubhouse. We'll get on the bus and I'll teach you the ropes of how we travel." I waited and waited and nobody came out of the clubhouse. Some 45 minutes had gone by and the media types and the personnel—basically everyone except for the team—was waiting to get on the bus. Like a dummy, I opened the door to the clubhouse. Nobody had undressed yet because Stanky was reeling—he hated losing, especially close games. There I was standing in the doorway. Stanky, who was very sarcastic, said, "May we help you, young man?" I wanted to crawl out of the goddamn place.

He continued, "Would you like to come over and sit by me?" Now I was really catching it. I figured the shit's going to hit the fan. Infielder Solly Hemus and outfielder Peanuts Lowrey were sitting over in the corner of the clubhouse trying to choke back their laughter because they knew I was going to get it. So I sat down. The club rule was that when the team lost, someone had to buy a box of cigars to pass around. There were 50 cigars in a box, and each had to cost at least 50 cents apiece. For 1954, that was a pretty good cigar.

The designee for that loss—as appointed by Stanky—was starting pitcher Vic Raschi. He had been a great pitcher for five straight World Series champions for Casey Stengel's Yankees from 1949-1953. Stanky asked Raschi to stand up, and then he said to him, "I understand, Mr. Raschi, that you are the designated buyer of the cigars for the night's loss. You know that it's your job now to designate the next buyer." Raschi picked right up on it and said, "I think Mr. Hamilton ought to buy the next box."

That moment broke the ice, and Stanky said to the team, "Okay, let's get dressed—let's get on the bus and go." For whatever reason, maybe because I took it like a man, Stanky took to me like a cat to a bowl of milk. When we got on the bus, he had me sit by him in the front row—a rare request for certain. That began a friendship between Stanky and me. He treated me like his own kid.

But Stanky was a Jekyll-and-Hyde-type person. Broeg and I would ride to the park in a cab with him, and I'd go up to the booth and drop off my briefcase, and Broeg would drop off his typewriter. Then we'd head back down to the field, where Stanky was already dressed and in the dugout. We would walk right into the dugout and Stanky would act like he didn't know either one of us—after we'd been with him all day. To him, when he put the uniform on, he was in another world.

Stanky truly knew the game of baseball. As a player, he was one of those little piss-pot infielders who would do anything to beat you. As a manager, he was a disciple of Leo Durocher, the legendary skipper who snapped the Yankees' string of titles in 1954 with the New York Giants. I wanted Stanky as a friend, but I appreciated him as a mentor, too. When I was curious about different things, he offered to answer my questions. I always found him helpful.

But his players didn't really like him a bit, because Stanky could be brash. In a game at the Polo Grounds against the Giants, we blew a big lead in the game. After the game, Broeg wrote his story and I finished up my duties. We left together for the clubhouse. At the Polo Grounds, the trip from the press box to the clubhouse was like an overnight hike; we had to walk through the infield and the outfield to reach the clubhouse, which was beyond the outfield wall past a little bleacher section. Well, when we got to left-center field, we could already hear Stanky yelling at his players. It was the day before the cutdown date. He said over and over again: "I don't know who's going tomorrow, but somebody's going." Then he said, "Maybe it will be Gertrude."

"Gertrude" was Stanky's nickname for pitcher Stu Miller, who went on to be a successful reliever for the Giants and the Orioles. It was an insulting nickname that Stanky gave Miller because Miller played bridge all the time and Stanky didn't like that. That's just the way he was. Sure enough, the next day Stu Miller was gone.

As much as I enjoyed my time with Stanky, the 1954 season was also memorable for negative reasons: it was the year my problems with Harry Caray began. Caray was a fixture, a big-time star broadcaster who had been in St. Louis for years. I had never met him but had heard of him and couldn't wait to meet him. I thought his enthusiastic approach to broadcasting was the kind of thing I could learn from. A lot of the old-time broadcasters—including my idol Bob Elson—were pretty much nuts-and-bolts guys, which most of the broadcasters were in the 1920s, '30s, and '40s.

I first met Caray at Keel Auditorium when we were working the same college basketball game. I was doing the TV, and he was doing the radio. Instead of saying to me, "Nice to meet you" or "Good luck to you," he said something negative: "Don't worry about it, kid. Nobody's going to be watching you tonight. They're all going to be listening to me on the radio." It was a lesson for me: Caray couldn't bring himself to treat someone in a nice way. He was just a paranoid person who didn't want anything good happening to anybody but himself. From the start, our pairing was hardly a match made in heaven.

I was hired by KXOX to travel on the road with Caray and help him out on the air. From the beginning, he wanted no part of me. I'll never forget how that 1954 season opened. At his re-introduction to me, he looked me right in the face and said, "Kid, don't worry about your mike being on because *I* am the announcer here." It was going to be a very long season, and it became obvious Caray was going to try to make me feel like a jackass.

Others saw it happening, too. Bob Broeg, the beat writer, M. Leo Ward, the team's traveling secretary, and Stanky each saw how poorly Caray treated me. Stanky hated Caray to begin with and Broeg didn't like him much either, because he didn't think Caray had been fair to Stan Musial. Broeg thought Musial hung the moon. When the Cardinals were struggling, which was often, Caray would get on a player and just keep it up. The year after I left, he practically ran Kenny Boyer out of town. In fact, Boyer challenged him in the locker room.

It was during my time with the Cardinals that Broeg, Ward, and Stanky—and some others—began referring to Caray as "the

Canary." I could see why, as Caray had a way of getting under your skin. During broadcasts, Caray would constantly second-guess Stanky. One instance in particular that really irked Stanky involved Harry Walker, who was managing one of our AAA teams while his brother Dixie Walker was managing another one. We were on the road and Caray was wailing about Stanky. "You know," he said on the air, "we've got Harry Walker leading by five games in Rochester. Dixie Walker's leading by seven in Columbus. And Johnny Keane's got his club playing well in Omaha. And here we are with Eddie Stanky wallowing in fifth place." Mrs. Stanky heard the criticism and told her husband. That was the straw that broke the camel's back for Stanky.

Stanky, Broeg, Ward, and I formed a tight bond partially because we all disliked Caray. We spent a lot of time together off the field. Stanky would have me get the newspaper for him so he could see the movie timetable. He was a whodunit movie guy who enjoyed solving the murder mysteries. So Broeg, Ward, Stanky, and I would all go out for lunch and then watch the movie that Stanky picked. In an afternoon movie, there were open seats all over the place. But Stanky wouldn't let anyone sit next to him. He made us take up a whole row, four seats apart.

In addition to the movies, Broeg, Ward, and Stanky took me to dinner and we went out after games. That's how I learned to really appreciate fine dining. What an experience that was for a kid from Iowa who'd never been to a nice restaurant in his life. And what a pleasant time that was compared to my time spent in the booth with Caray.

I had plenty of additional reasons to be excited that season. I took my first plane ride with the team on an old TWA Constellation. Other than that one trip, we always traveled by train, which I loved. Riding the train was a part of the romance of baseball. I got to enjoy the camaraderie on the team and the organization as a whole. The best part of the whole experience was listening to players talk about baseball, hearing them discuss strategy, and even share batting tips with each other. Believe me, when Red Schoendienst and Stan Musial were giving advice, people listened. It was nothing to see a star player get up inside the train, show off his batting stance, and give a rookie a few pointers. Even the baseball writers would get to observe. All of that is missing today in baseball. Today's ballplayer either goes to sleep, watches a movie, or plays cards. But back in the '50s, they just talked baseball all the time.

On the trains, the players shared time and space with the media as if they were roommates, which gave the players a better feel for the reporters who would critique them in the papers. The players knew that anything heard or seen on those train rides by the media was not going to be news in tomorrow's paper. That was an unstated rule. The baseball beat writers covered baseball only, and most of that occurred on the field.

Sports coverage on television wasn't established yet in the early 1950s, so beat writers didn't have to compete with coverage on the TV. Back then, the beat writer would just knock out the facts of the game, and then he was done and could sit back and enjoy himself. And we all enjoyed the train rides—especially the service we received.

If we boarded the train at midnight after a game, the railroad had to add on a dining car so that the players could eat at that late hour. For this service, the team was charged $2,000.

As we left on one late-night trip, Ward, the traveling secretary, said, "Guys, tonight's one of the nights when they had to put on a dining car. You know it cost me two grand. I know you can't eat the two grand, but eat all you can of it." In those days we were receiving $7.50 a day in meal money. So we took advantage of the all-you-can-eat buffet. Some of the players ordered two or three steaks and ice cream by the gallon. It was a treat.

On the train, each of us had our own little roomette—a private sleeping car. There was a little trap door under the sink for our shoes. While we were sleeping, the porter shined the shoes and put them back into the slot. If we got into a town at four or five in the morning, we didn't get off the train. They pulled the train off to the side and we slept till eight, allowing us to get a full night's sleep. Then they got us up, put us on the team bus, and took us to the hotel.

If there's one thing I wish I could change today, I would prefer that teams travel more by train. I really miss those old train rides. The company was enjoyable, and it was a unique way to discover America.

Train rides aside, the best thing about working for the Cardinals was seeing Stan Musial play every day. Musial was my hero. I rooted for him when he came up in the early '40s, followed his career and meteoric rise to stardom, and then got a chance to see him in action on a regular basis. Nobody ever said a bad word about Musial. He was a gracious, generous man. I've got a trophy case at home with an autographed ball from both Stan the Man and Red Schoendienst. They're in the same case because I think it's unique that the pair—who were roommates together while with the Cardinals—both became Hall of Famers. They were both class guys.

But I only had that one season to watch Musial play. At the end of the 1954 season, the club wanted to go back to the old formula that Caray had employed with the late Gabby Street and Gus Mancuso. Caray wanted an old-time player as his broadcast partner. Joe Garagiola was a big name in St. Louis. He had grown up there with Yogi Berra and had played for the Cardinals in the late 1940s and early 1950s. Plus, Garagiola had shown some inclination to be a good broadcaster because of his natural humor. So the team picked him. I couldn't disagree, as the move actually made sense: Garagiola was a St. Louis figure.

But the Cardinals didn't forget about me. In those days, they had 24 farm teams, including Triple-A clubs in Omaha, Columbus, and Rochester. They said I could have my pick. I liked Rochester because they were the most successful of the farm teams at the time, and Bing Devine was their general manager. In my interview with him, however, Devine said that I asked for too much money. So I wasn't sure that job was going to come through.

In the meantime, I was going home to Iowa every winter to do the Iowa high school basketball tournament. While I was there, Jim Zobel of WHO in Des Moines, who had broadcast Iowa prep games for 50 years, asked what I was planning to do the next year. I said, "I'm not sure, I may go to Rochester and do Triple-A games.

I'd like to stay in the big leagues if I can, but if I go to AAA, at least I'll still be in baseball."

He said he received a call from a friend at WIND in Chicago who told him they were looking for a guy to travel with Burt Wilson, who did the Cubs games at that time. I was definitely interested, to say the least.

6

BANKING ON THE CUBS

My audition for WIND in Chicago was held inside the Wrigley Building on Michigan Avenue. In my audition, I had to prove to them that I was a flexible announcer. If I got the job, the station might ask me to read the news and host a record show, then head out to broadcast a baseball game. In those old days, a broadcaster had to be ready for anything. Hence, during my audition, I had to read some opera because they were still using the same audition scripts that they had used in the 1930s and 1940s. I remember reading the opera introduction, and the folks at WIND sort of laughed in response. Then I prepared a five-minute newscast, because the station did news twice every hour. Finally, I was asked to introduce some new records, in case I had to host a rock 'n' roll show on the air. Little did I know then that I would be doing just that in a few years.

Back then, it was common to work 12-14 hours a day. WIND had been the flagship station for a long time and was owned by Ralph Atlas of the famous Atlas broadcasting family. The interview and the audition went well. Soon after I finished my audition, they said, "We like you—do you want to come?" And I said, "Hell, yes." It was good timing for them, since spring training had already started and the start of the 1955 season wasn't too far away.

I was excited to get to work with Cubs announcer Burt Wilson. I already knew a little bit about him because he got his start broadcasting baseball games in Cedar Rapids, Iowa, in the 1930s. We didn't meet, however, until 1950. While I was working my first post-college job at WQUA in Moline, Illinois, I went to Chicago and Burt invited me to sit in his booth during a Cubs game. In the seventh inning, he turned around to me and asked, "Would you like to do an inning?" *Would I like to do an inning?* I didn't even need a cab to get back to my hotel after the game; I was floating. I just did an inning of a big-league game!

That year at WIND, I did everything but sweep out the joint. I had to be there at six in the morning to read commercials on the Howard Miller disc jockey show. Through Miller's show, I earned a following right away. Miller had the biggest audience in Chicago, and was the biggest DJ in the country. To be honest, I probably received more recognition for my work on that morning show than I received working afternoon Cubs games with Burt Wilson. In addition to the morning gig, I did a commuter show each day from 5-6 p.m., took two hours off, and then was back on the air from 8-10 p.m. playing rock 'n' roll each night. It was a full day to say the least.

Those commercials on Miller's show put some additional money in my pocket. I also made a bundle of money every year at the big auto show at Chicago's McCormick Place. Ford Automobiles would hire me every year to talk about their cars as they rotated around and around on a platform. Looking back, it was because of those experiences that the commercial business became a large part of my career.

I did two live music shows in the morning on Miller's show with a boy and girl singer and a piano player. Then I caught the

Milo has interviewed plenty of famous players, but possibly none more prestigious than Jackie Robinson. Here Milo interviews Robinson at Wrigley Field in 1956.

El—Chicago's above-ground subway—to Wrigley Field to help Burt do the game. About the seventh inning I'd leave, because I had to go back down to the station to do the scoreboard show, and then do a record show from 5-6 p.m. for evening drive. When the team was on the road, I traveled with Burt.

Burt was an interesting broadcasting partner. He was not necessarily a ladies man, but he liked to *look*. He always had his binoculars out in the press box so he could scan the stands. I remember on one particular day he was looking out toward the leftfield bleachers and he remarked, "You know Milo, I've been watching this one young couple in the front row of the bleachers all day and I finally figured out what they're doing: He's kissing her the strikes." He just let it hang there.

In those days, Burt did Cubs baseball, Bears football, and other things at the radio station and was making $25,000 in salary. I broke in at WIND and was making $145 a week, but then I would get extra money for doing commercials or other add-on assignments. I'd make $7.50 for a commercial, and by the end of the year I had over $2,000 extra coming my way. We had to hustle in those days to make a living, believe me.

We weren't the only ones hustling, either. Guests on our Cubs pregame show would get $20 each, which was a lot back then. I remember one time I interviewed Stan Musial on the pregame show and handed him $20. He waved me off, saying, "I don't need that. Give it to the clubhouse guy." But that sort of attitude was a rarity. There were a few guys who wouldn't come on for that kind of money—they wanted more. Leo Durocher was one of them. Remember, he had been in New York and had been courted by the best there. He'd tell me, "I don't do anything for less than $1,000." That was his way of telling me to go away.

I remember the time then-Pirates manager Bobby Bragan was on the show. The Pirates had just called up this young second baseman named Bill Mazeroski. "He's never going back," Bragan told me, with confidence, "and he's going to be the greatest fielding second baseman you'll ever see." He was right on target.

Despite being on the air for several years, Wilson had stage fright. As the time would near for our broadcast to begin, Burt would become as nervous as a whore in church. He'd say to me, "When we get close to going on, you open up and I'll take it from there." But Wilson was an enthusiastic broadcaster, and he had his own charm, like his slogan: "It's never over 'til the last man is out."

After the '55 season, Wilson was offered a job with the Cincinnati Reds. The Reds were going to televise 30 games a year in 1956 and they asked Burt to be their television announcer. He was hired for $30,000, which was $5,000 more than he had ever made—not bad for 30 games. Before he started his new job, however, Burt needed to visit the doctor for some self-assurance.

Wilson was a hypochondriac, and every year at the All-Star break he thought there was something physically wrong with him. So, instead of taking the three days off during the All-Star break, he would check into Illinois Masonic Hospital to see if a doctor could find anything wrong or just give him some peace of mind. He went back home to Mesa, Arizona following the 1955 season, to his new home near the Cubs training facility. When he arrived that December, he asked his doctor to really give him a good physical because he had a new job in Cincinnati and he wanted to be certain of his health. Wilson checked into the hospital and they ran all kinds of tests. By late in the afternoon, the doctor came by and told him everything looked good. The only thing he noticed was that Burt still had slightly high blood pressure, but he assured Burt that he would be all right with the medicine he had been taking to control it. The doctor then suggested that Burt spend the night at the hospital and go home in the morning. The next morning he was dead; Wilson died in the middle of the night from a heart attack. He was only in his early forties.

Jack Quinlan was given Wilson's job with the Cubs, and so I worked with Jack beginning in the 1956 season. There were three of us working on the broadcasts, including Gene Elston, who later did Astros games for 25 years. After the 1957 season, the team shifted to WGN, which had won the broadcast rights from WIND. Jack Brickhouse knew Quinlan from Peoria, where he had done Bradley basketball. Quinlan got a job on the WGN crew with Brickhouse and they decided to give my spot to a player. That was Lou Boudreau, who was best known as the player-manager of the 1948 World Champion Indians.

But no matter who broadcast for those Cubs, they couldn't help the team. The Cubs of the mid-'50s were led by Ernie Banks and some decent bats such as Dee Fondy, Hank Sauer, Walt Moryn, Cal Neeman, and Gene Baker. But the club didn't have much depth and had poor pitching. The 1955 team finished sixth, 26 games out, under manager Stan Hack. The 1956 team finished dead last, 33 games out. Then, in 1957, Bob Scheffing took over as skipper, and the team again finished 33 games out, tied for last, at 62-92. You can imagine what those three years were like in the broadcast booth. We had a lot of time to fill, and often we had to be a bit creative.

Banks was the centerpiece of the Cubs in those days, a terrific ballplayer with a great personality off the field. There were some folks who thought he was always putting them on with his constant smile and his happy attitude. I get asked that a lot, "How did Ernie remain so upbeat while his team was losing?" Well, that

Milo presents Mr. Cub, Ernie Banks, with an award during a pregame show in 1956.

was just the kind of person Ernie was. He was always optimistic, always positive.

Ernie had his back-to-back MVP years in 1958-'59, so I wasn't around for those years, but we could tell early on that he was going to earn some notoriety as a slugging shortstop. He wasn't some mediocre-hitting, slick-fielding shortstop. He was an adequate fielder, but hitting was his game. Not many remember that the White Sox tried to sign him, and I've often wondered what might have happened if they signed him instead of the Cubs. You might not have heard as much about Banks, because the old Comiskey Park had dimensions in the outfield that ran halfway to the lake. Wrigley Field was different. That ballpark's power alley was in left centerfield, a perfect fit for Banks. His righthanded swing was grooved for that spot in left center, and I'm sure it added 200 home

runs to his career. Even so, I never guessed he would hit 512 career home runs and wind up in the Hall of Fame. But he was the kind of hitter who was so consistent that he got his 40 or so homers almost every season.

Gene Baker, the Cubs' second baseman at that time, and Banks both got their start in the big leagues during the 1953 season. They were a perfect combination in the infield. Baker, who was a much better fielder than Ernie, helped Banks on defense. And together, the two of them didn't feel as alone on an island at a time when racial integration in the major leagues was still rough around the edges.

That's how I felt when the Cubs job disappeared: alone on an island.

After the 1957 season, I had two children—Patti Joy and Mark—and my wife, Arlene, but no baseball job. WIND in Chicago asked me to stay on at the station and spin records. This may come as a shock to those who know me only as a baseball broadcaster, but there are some guys in the record promotion business who will tell you to this day that I should be in the Rock 'n' Roll Hall of Fame. After the Cubs let me go, I made a significant transition in my career and became a nighttime disc jockey.

From 1958 to 1961, I did all the rock 'n' roll record hops. When singers Bobby Darin or Connie Francis came to Chicago, we'd have them on the show. When Jackie DeShannon, The Platters, or Bobby Rydell were in town playing a concert, they stopped by the studio. During that time, I also became very close with Nat King Cole, because his promotion man, Dick LaPalm, was a big fan of mine.

Since I had made the major leagues in 1953, this four-year period proved to be the only years during my career that I did not cover major league baseball. I loved being a disc jockey, but I wanted to get back into baseball again. But that period of time was good for me, and I was happy with my situation.

Finally, a baseball opportunity came in the summer of 1961. It was a case of being in the right place at the right time. Ed Wallace, the station's general manager, asked me to come down to WIND and have lunch with him. Well, we *never* had lunch together, so I suspected that something was up. I got to his office and he said, "Milo, we're changing formats here, and we're going to have to let you go. But you don't have to leave today. When would you like to leave?" I was upset. I replied, "It's 11:50, so how would noon be?"

I was out of work but felt like a weight had been lifted off my shoulders. I told myself, "Now you can go do what you want to do—baseball." And to show you there were no hard feelings between Wallace and me, years later he would be the same guy who would bring me to Pittsburgh to replace Bob Prince at KDKA. I came to realize that Wallace was really doing me a favor. He knew that I wanted to be back in baseball, and I think he got me moving in that direction. Besides, he gave me a big severance package when I left WIND.

It turned out I was only unemployed a few days. Bob Finnegan, who had worked with Burt Wilson back in the 1940s, was now the program director at WCFL, the White Sox station. Finnegan said he didn't have an opening yet for baseball but wanted me to come to the station and host an afternoon record show because they needed a summer replacement. I accepted, and it was a good move on my part.

In those days, WCFL was also re-creating other American League games, and I became involved with those as well. Those re-creation days bring back fond memories—and some interesting stories, too. For example, during one game I reported six runs scoring in a particular inning, only to get a "correction" from Western Union minutes later that only *four runs* had actually scored. So I had to find a creative way to "erase" two runs off the board, just like that. Despite those sort of challenges, I hadn't broadcast a baseball game in almost four years, and the itch was still there.

By the end of the 1961 season, Ralph Kiner, the great slugger who had been doing the White Sox color work with the great Bob Elson at WCFL, informed the station that he was going to the Mets

to join Lindsey Nelson and Bob Murphy in a group that would have a long run in New York. Although many thought that Bob Rhodes—who had been at the station waiting in the wings—would get the job of replacing Kiner at WCFL, Finnegan liked me better. He said my voice just "sounded" like a baseball announcer's voice. He gave me the nod, and re-started my career as a baseball announcer.

7

CHANGING MY SOX

I joined the White Sox in 1962 and enjoyed four good years there. Coming over to the White Sox was a nice transition; I had known Bob Elson, or "The Commander" as he was called, for many years and certainly was up to date on the "Go-Go Sox" and their star players Luis Aparicio, Early Wynn, and Nellie Fox. Prior to joining the team, I had done a few White Sox games on Mutual Radio, with Bob Feller doing the color, so I had kept up with them.

It was a spirited team, led by manager Al Lopez, a fellow who had directed the Cleveland Indians to the 1954 World Series. He had started with the White Sox in 1957 and would be there through the 1965 season, also returning in 1968-'69. He had steered the White Sox close to a World Series win in 1959, but ultimately lost to the Los Angeles Dodgers. Lopez was the kind of man who *looked* the part of a businessman. He always wore a tie and would dress up away from the baseball field. When we traveled, he just looked the part of somebody *important*. And he was married to a Broadway showgirl. He had a presence you couldn't forget.

In those days, four Chicago papers—the *Tribune*, the *American*, the *Sun-Times* and the *Daily News*—partially covered the White Sox. At the All-Star break, a paper would cover the White Sox the first half and then switch to the Cubs for the second half of the season (or vice versa). The papers wouldn't cover the team for the whole season.

One of the beat writers for the *Daily News*, John Carmichael, was a heavy drinker and had a column called "the Barber's Pole." It even had a picture of a striped barber's pole. Carmichael was amazing. He *never* took a note during the game, yet he remembered all of the details. I would see him in the dugout interviewing a player or Lopez without a pen, pencil, or notepad. And then he would write a terrific story or column the next day. He was considered one of the best writers of his time and later won the J.G. Taylor Spink award, which honors baseball's best writers every year. Warren Brown, who wrote for the *American*, also won the award. They were good baseball writers, as were fellow Chicago scribes Edgar Munzel and Jerome Holtzman. That's four guys out of the same era who were a great group to be around.

Speaking of great people to be around—my partner in the broadcast booth sure was an interesting guy. Elson was a gin hustler. Wherever we traveled on the road, Elson had guys in town who wanted to play gin with him. They didn't care how much money they lost, they just enjoyed being able to brag about playing cards with him.

Those same people were willing to lose money to one-time White Sox and Orioles skipper Paul Richards just to be able to say that they played golf with him. Elson was playing gin with the Sox players one time when Richards was managing the Go-Go White Sox in the early 1950s. Guys were losing money when they couldn't afford to, so Richards finally put his foot down and told Elson to stop playing cards with his team.

Elson's trick was simple: he would talk you to death, causing his opponents to lose their concentration and make silly mistakes. He sure did make a lot of money playing gin. But the one guy he couldn't beat was Al Lopez. A pretty good gin player himself, Lopez was sick and tired of hearing Elson brag about his prowess at cards. About twice a year he'd say, "Bob, can we play a little gin?" And he'd beat Bob's pants off. But then Elson would never pay Lopez. He could never figure out why he couldn't beat him.

One of Elson's targets was Holtzman, who wanted to learn how to play gin in the worst way. On one road trip, Holtzman—who was called "Tammy" by Elson—was practically begging for a gin rummy lesson on the plane. Finally, Bob says, "One of these days, my boy." So a few weeks later on a long charter flight home, I heard a voice about four rows behind me, "Ohhhh, Tammy, Tammy." Holtzman looked back, "Yes, Bob." And Elson replied, "Come back and join me, it's time for your lessons to begin," adding "and I want to advise you that these are going to be *very, very, very* expensive lessons."

I enjoyed Holtzman's company a lot because we were both young guys who broke in together in Chicago, and we were kind of cheering for each other in our given professions. I don't even know why Elson called Holtzman "Tammy," but I'm probably the only guy alive now who still calls him by that nickname. Elson didn't mean it to be derogatory. It was just a name he pinned on him.

The White Sox teams of the early '60s had two very good men up the middle of the field and batting first and second in the order in Luis Aparicio and Nellie Fox. When I first joined the broadcast team in 1962, Fox took me under his wing. In those days, the team played father-son games once a season. At the time, they didn't allow the girls to play. Fox had two daughters but didn't have a son, so Nellie would always ask my son Mark to join him in these contests. Fox's nickname was "Muggsy," and all the players starting calling my son "Little Muggs." The nickname stuck with Mark for years, even after he grew up to be about 6-4 and 265 pounds. He was always Little Muggs.

Nellie was only there with me during the 1962 and '63 seasons. He had a bit of a falling out with the Sox at the end of his career. He thought that the organization would hire him as a manager for their Triple A team in Indianapolis, but they declined. So he went off to Houston, then called the Colt .45s, and finished the final two seasons of his 19-year career. After his playing days he became a coach for both Gil Hodges and Ted Williams in Washington. But Nellie never got to manage himself, and that was a surprise to me. He would have made a very good manager, but he died from brain cancer far too young, at the age of 48 in 1975.

As a player, Fox was a lot like Bill Mazeroski. Both got into the Hall of Fame on their fielding skills, although Fox used to annoy the heck out of Lopez with the way he took the throw on a double play in *front* of second base. But Nellie was one of the greats and truly deserved to be in the Hall, just like Maz. Lopez never voted for him on the veterans committee for induction into the Hall of Fame. There was a rumor that he and Nellie didn't get along. All I know is that as good a player as Nellie was, somewhere along the line he must have ticked off Lopez. Al didn't like him, and to carry that situation a step further, I remember that when Nellie finally was voted in—after his death—Mrs. Fox never thanked or mentioned Lopez at the induction ceremonies in Cooperstown.

The other part of that great infield double-play combination was Aparicio, a player who always had the knack for making things happen on the ball field. You loved him as your leadoff hitter, because Looie was a guy who would steal 50 or more bases in a season. And he was a Gold Glove shortstop, just a gem as a player. Looking back, I was really fortunate during my Chicago years to have an opportunity to watch both Banks and then Aparicio. Same thing for the second basemen I witnessed in Chicago, first Fox and later Ryne Sandberg.

The 1964 White Sox should have gone to the World Series. That season, Gary Peters won 20 and Juan Pizarro racked up 19 victories. Add in Hoyt Wilhelm, Joe Horlen, and John Buzhardt, and it really was a solid pitching staff. Elson would often introduce the knuckleballer Wilhelm by saying, "Here comes Dr. Wilhelm and his dancing medicine show."

Prior to Opening Day in 1962, three future Hall of Famers—Nellie Fox, Milo, and Luis Aparicio—smile for the camera.

Our shortstop in '64, Ron Hansen, was nicknamed "The Horn" because he had a rather distinguished beak for a nose. We used to say that if a pitcher ever hit him in the nose, it would be a double to right. Hansen came over from Baltimore along with Wilhelm in a trade that sent Aparicio to the Orioles. Hansen was a big shortstop, in the mold of Marty Marion, and he was a real clutch hitter. Had statisticians kept track of the game-winning RBI stat back then, Hansen would have been up near the top during several of his seasons with the Sox. He was one of those players who got hits when it *meant* something. And he had 20-home-run power, too.

Pete Ward, our third baseman, was another clutch player. He led the team with 23 homers and 94 RBI that season. Dave Nicholson, an outfielder, provided power, too, but struck out way too often. Overall, however, we weren't a particularly powerful club.

Camilo Carreon, one of the catchers, was a guy who often got under the skin of Lopez, who had been a pretty fair major-league catcher himself. Carreon drove Lopez nuts because he'd always catch with his glove hand pointing down. Lopez was forever on him, and one time decided to teach him a lesson by benching him in favor of Smoky Burgess, who was grabbed off waivers from Pittsburgh and was nearing the end of his career. Of course, Lopez wasn't doing ol' Smoky any favors by giving him a start, because by that time in his career, Burgess was pretty much an exclusive pinch-hitter—and a good one. For one game, Lopez started Burgess, and Smoky was dying out there behind the plate. Even in his prime, Smoky hadn't looked like he was in shape. So Al had to get the old guy out of there by the sixth inning. That lesson lasted only one game.

The summer of '64 was especially exciting, with the Sox battling Baltimore and the Yankees down the stretch. The Orioles had Brooks Robinson and Boog Powell, and pitchers Wally Bunker, Milt Pappas, and Robin Roberts. The Yankees, managed by Yogi Berra, still featured the M & M Boys—Mickey Mantle and Roger Maris—along with Tom Tresh, Joe Pepitone, and a pitching staff led by Jim Bouton, Whitey Ford, and Al Downing. They also got some late-season help from rookie Mel Stottlemyre. Without Stottlemyre in September, the White Sox probably would have reached the World Series.

We went into Yankee Stadium in August and swept a doubleheader. Not long after that came the famous Phil Linz harmonica incident on the Yankee team bus. Phil upset the Yankee coaches by playing "Mary Had a Little Lamb" on his harmonica after a loss. First-year manager Yogi Berra stormed to the back of the bus and threw the harmonica in disgust. Lots of media thought that event might send the Yankees into a dive. It appeared that might be the case when the Bombers came to our place and we swept all four games. By the end of the day on August 20, we led the Orioles by a half-game and New York by four and a half games.

In those days, teams played doubleheaders most Sundays and on holidays. That was 30 scheduled doubleheaders during a season, and with rainouts, possibly 40 doubleheaders in six months! Looking back, I think all those doubleheaders finally took a toll on the White Sox down the stretch in 1964.

We took the division lead after playing a Labor Day doubleheader, with the second game going extra innings. It was a long day, and to make matters worse we had to fly out right after the game to Washington to play the next day, a "twi-nighter" on September 7. I don't think we got to bed until 4 a.m., so we were beat. We sure looked like we were sleepwalking against the Senators. I mean we faced two pitchers in the doubleheader who hadn't won but a handful of games between them since May. But Benny Daniels and Jim Duckworth ended up beating us twice. And just to show it wasn't a fluke, 11 days later, the Senators visited Chicago and the *same* two guys pitched and beat us again.

The Senators were a horrible team, losing 100 games that season, and the White Sox never recovered. They didn't exactly fall apart—going 19-11 down the stretch—but the Yankees went 27-9 over the same period.

How did Lopez handle the late-season slide? He was disappointed, but unlike Earl Weaver and Billy Martin, Al wasn't a ranter and a raver. He was a damn good umpire baiter, though. He'd get on the umps pretty good and a lot of the umpires didn't like him. Lopez was tough, one of those silent, leading types of managers. He didn't ride players hard, but everyone *knew* who the manager was. If something went wrong, he'd call that player into his office and let him have it. But Lopez never embarrassed a player in the clubhouse or in front of the media. It wasn't his style.

Guys who played for Lopez hold him in the highest regard— they still refer to him as *Mr.* Lopez. It reminds me of how players respected legendary Philadelphia Athletics manager Connie Mack.

Al had a good bunch of coaches surrounding him, and he always brought the same group along wherever he went. Tony Cuccinello, a funny guy, was the third base coach. He was Al's golfing partner when they lived across the street from each other in Tampa. Those two played golf every day. After golf, they'd play gin rummy at the country club. The other coaches were Don Gutteridge, Ray Berres, and Johnny Cooney.

The greatest pitching coach–manager combination that I was ever associated with was Berres and Lopez. And the funny thing about it was they were both catchers. But they could teach and they knew how to handle a pitching staff. Lopez's White Sox teams didn't score a lot of runs, so he relied on strong pitching to keep him in the division race every year. Berres was a great pitching coach because he was a student of the game—and he was an excellent instructor. It didn't matter if it was a veteran pitcher or a rookie, you always saw Ray in the bullpen discussing various grips and techniques. He would catch his pitchers in the bullpen between starts and sometimes prior to the game. He wanted to know just what that pitcher had that day, so he could tell Al. You don't see that anymore. Now, each club has a bullpen catcher.

My last year with the White Sox was 1965, and we were coming off a very good season. The 1965 team was good, winning 95 games and finishing seven games back of Minnesota. That team featured Joel Horlen, Gary Peters, a young Tommy John, and two knuckleball relievers, Hoyt Wilhelm and Eddie Fisher. There were also some new faces on that ball club, with Bill "Moose" Skowron at first base, Don Buford at second, Ken Berry in center, Danny Cater in left, Johnny Romano at catcher, and Floyd Robinson in right. It was a real solid team, but Minnesota had it going that season and proved to be too much.

Teaming with Elson in the booth during the '60s was a real pleasure. What made us a great broadcasting team, I believe, was that some regarded me as a "Bob Elson with enthusiasm," and it offered White Sox fans a nice contrast during the broadcasts. I loved to keep stats, and Bob saw all the detailed books of information that I kept. I didn't mind doing a lot of the grunt work, believe me. I would keep the score sheets and do the pregame and postgame reports, giving out scores of other games from around the league from the information I got off the Western Union ticker. I was a real jack-of-all-trades and I enjoyed all the work.

I think Elson realized early on how much I revered him, and he knew that I was devoted to the broadcast by all the information that I kept and shared with him. I even kept a home-run stats book, detailing all of the homers hit by the opposition and the White Sox, off what pitcher, dates, et cetera. I fed Elson all of those tidbits on the air again and again. And I'm sure he figured if I was willing to share all that background work, I must be a pretty good kid. The way I saw it, I was just being a teammate, and that's what made our partnership work out so well.

We genuinely enjoyed each other's company, especially our dinners on the road trips. It didn't matter to me that Elson was one of the most notorious freeloaders the game had ever seen, either. He was an All-Star, and we always ate well as a result. I remember the time we went to Al Schacht's restaurant in New York. Schacht was a close friend of the great hurler Walter Johnson and had a 53-game career in the big leagues cut short by injury. After his baseball career, he got into the entertainment business and became well known as "The Clown Prince of Baseball."

Whenever we went to Yankee Stadium, I knew that Schacht was going to be the guest on the pregame show. I mean, that was a given. After the game, Al would take Elson and me back to our hotels, where he'd drop Elson off at the Plaza and me at the Roosevelt. Elson got to stay in the first-class hotel, a deal he cut with the team and the station. That's the perk you get for being the No. 1 announcer. On most of our trips into New York City, we would arrange to meet at Al's restaurant at seven for dinner, and normally Elson would be a few minutes late . . . for a good reason I was to find out.

Al's restaurant also featured a big bar, so Bob and I would stop and have a drink before dinner. Elson would order Beefeater martinis and I drank Tanqueray. Elson had this great line when ordering his drink, and he did it with every bartender who ever waited on him. "Well, waiter, I would like a *very, very, very, very dry* Beefeater's martini with three olives and on the rocks, and it better be that dry or you're gonna drink it."

After a couple of drinks, it was time for dinner. In those days—unlike now—everyone ate steak and potatoes. Elson had real bad teeth, so he couldn't chew well enough to eat a good steak. Elson would ask Schacht, "Al, do you suppose your chefs could grind up one of those nice steaks and make me a hamburger patty?" Well, the look on Al's face broke his heart, knowing one of his prime steaks was going to be ground into a hamburger patty for Bob, but he invariably would grant this wish and send the order back to the chef.

Just before leaving the restaurant, we'd go upstairs to the third floor of the building—where Schacht lived—to visit with Al's wife, who was Irish. Schacht was Jewish, and he'd call his wife his Irish Rose. They had a little Boston terrier, and boy could that dog talk. Elson owned a few French poodles, and he just loved dogs. So we'd be sitting up in Al's apartment and Elson would get so excited by talking to this goddamn dog. That normally went on for 15 or 20 minutes, and then—timing things perfectly—he would turn to Schacht and say, "Al, well we gotta get to the theatre and we're running a bit late. Can your limo driver take us?" Now we had our *free* limo ride. On the way downstairs, Elson would turn to me and yell, "Milo, take care of the waiter, take care of the bartender, and I'll go outside and hold the limo." I remember it like it was yesterday, dropping $5 bills for tips all over that restaurant. I knew what my job was.

I also didn't mind picking up the tab because we would also get free tickets to the theatre, left for us by J.G. Taylor Spink of *The Sporting News*. We saw some of the best Broadway plays in New York on someone else's tab. As we pulled up to the theater, Bob would say, "Milo, take care of the limo driver, I'm gonna jump out and get our tickets." We go inside and sit down and watch the play. At intermission, they would always serve the patrons orange juice. Of course, Elson asked me to get the orange juice while he went off to the restroom. Then we'd meet back in the lobby and invariably Elson would tell me he hated the play, or that he was tired or bored, and would then ask to go back to the hotel. I would reply, "Bob, this is a *wonderful* play. What's wrong with it?" And he would pause, think for a second, and then counter, "Oh, okay, we'll stay."

Bob Elson with Milo shortly after Elson was inducted into the Baseball Hall of Fame in 1979.

That was just his way of squeezing some free orange juice out of me. This act continued all night, long after we left the theatre and were en route back to the hotel in a cab. We would drop off Elson first, and along the way, Bob would say in a very loud voice so the cabbie could hear, "Well, what about it, you sonofabitch. I *treat* you to a nice steak dinner at Al Schacht's, I take you to a *great* Broadway theatre play, we have *wonderful* drinks . . . and you haven't even said thank you." That was classic Bob Elson at his best.

Elson always had a caddy—a guy who would carry his briefcase, come to the station, take him to the ballpark, or pick him up at the airport after a road trip. And he never paid the guy in cash. He gave him tickets to games and cigars. One of his caddies back in the '50s was Vince Garrity, who later became a big man in Chicago Mayor Richard Daley's regime as a politician. On one occasion, Garrity arrived about a quarter of six to pick Elson up for a sports show he had to do on WCFL at six o'clock. Elson said to Garrity, "As soon as I get through with the show, Vince, you gotta drive me out to Joliet. I'm speaking to an Old Timers dinner." Vince protested, "Bob, it's six o'clock, I've gotta go home." Bob replied, "Vince, I'll tell you what I'm going to do. Drive me out to Joliet and I'm going to give you half of what they give me." In those days, Vince figured he had to do it. So they drove out to Joliet.

While they were waiting for dessert to be served, Elson got up to go to the men's room just as the chairman of the dinner stopped by his table. The chairman said to Garrity, "I know you brought Mr. Elson out tonight. Here's the envelope with his honorarium." There were six $50 bills in there, and in the late '50s that was pretty good pay for a dinner speech. So Garrity opened up the envelope and took two out and put them in his pocket. When the dinner was over, Elson and Garrity were driving home and Garrity said, "Oh, by the way, the chairman came by and here's your honorarium." Elson opened the envelope and didn't say a word the rest of the drive home. He got out of the car, threw a $50 bill at Garrity, and said, "Would you believe those cheap sons-of-bitches only gave me $100?" Garrity still got his $150.

That was Elson, a wonderful man but an All-Star freeloader in a class all by himself. But hey, I was just very proud to be working with the guy. He was a pioneer in the sports radio business and had broadcast 14 All-Star games. I was happy to be along for the ride.

When Bob died at the age of 76 in 1981, I went to his wake. As a Methodist, I wasn't quite sure how the Catholics handled wakes, but Jack Brickhouse motioned for me to come out into the parlor area, away from the casket. He wanted me to tell Bob Elson stories—at his wake! That kind of thing happened a lot to me over the years. It seemed every time I visited Chicago, someone would ask me to tell the same Elson stories all over again or do my spot-on Elson impersonation. And of course, I obliged.

8

HAMMERIN' HANK AND ERNIE TOO

O n their way home from spring training each year, the White Sox always played exhibition games in the state of Georgia—at Macon, Savannah, and Atlanta. When we played in Atlanta in the spring of 1965, the fans there had more to look forward to than us stopping by next spring. By the time the 1965 season began, the Braves were a lame duck in Milwaukee and were all set to move to Atlanta the following season. So baseball fans in Atlanta already knew the Braves were coming the next year. In preparation, they formed a booster club called the Braves 400 and held a big luncheon at the Americana Hotel.

I was in town for the spring training game, so I stopped by the luncheon. When they introduced me to the audience, I received a terrific reception because the audience was already familiar with me from White Sox broadcasts. At that time, the White Sox had 90 to 100 stations in their network, which stretched all the way to

Florida. The Sox station in Atlanta was WGST, the Georgia Tech station.

After the luncheon, John McHale and Bill Bartholomay, the two top guys with the Braves, came up to the booth to visit with Bob Elson and me. They told me, "Boy, you got some kind of a welcome today. You ought to move down here with us next year." And that was where our conversation ended.

About three months later, a guy named Jim Faszhold called me. We had worked in the newsroom together when I was at the television station KTVI in St. Louis back in 1953. The Braves had hired him to set up their radio network throughout the Southeast. It was now 1965, and I hadn't heard from or even known where he was since 1953.

Jim told me, "John McHale and Bill Bartholomay hired me today to leave St. Louis and form their new network for them, get all these cities lined up. They told me my first job was to hire you as the announcer. I've looked at your schedule, and you're going to be in New York in a couple of weeks. We'd like to come and see you when the White Sox are there playing the Yankees."

That got the ball rolling. The White Sox had told me that I was going to be the heir-apparent to Bob Elson. But there really wasn't any retirement in sight for Bob, so I had to consider this a legitimate opportunity. I ended up accepting their offer and wound up announcing Hank Aaron's 715th home run nine years later, in 1974.

Ironically, I had helped broadcast Aaron's first home run as a visiting announcer with the Cardinals. It came in Milwaukee County Stadium against Vic Raschi, who had just been traded a few days earlier from the Yankees to the Cardinals. Aaron was not supposed to be with the '54 Braves, but Bobby Thomson had broken his ankle during the spring, and manager Charlie Grimm liked Aaron's bat. He had been an All-Star second baseman in every league he'd played in, but the Braves decided to put him in left field. I never thought he would become such a slugger. As a youth, he had grown up hitting cross-handed and had never shown that kind of power. Despite having 398 career home runs by the end of 1965, it wasn't until Aaron saw the Atlanta ballpark and heard about

Milo presents Hank Aaron with an award in the late 1960s.

the altitude of the city that he thought he had a chance at Babe Ruth's record.

In Milwaukee, Hank hit a lot of balls to right-center. But when he moved to Atlanta, he became a dead pull hitter. Watching him play every day during my first year with the Braves, I knew that he was something special because of the way the ball jumped off his bat. Yet, as good a hitter as Aaron was in Atlanta, until he announced for the first time in '72 that he was going after the career home run record, I don't think anybody really talked about it or thought about it. Everybody thought that Ruth's record was there to stay. Ruth himself thought 714 would never be broken. He thought that his single-season mark of 60 home runs would be broken because Jimmie Foxx, Hank Greenberg, and Hack Wilson had all come close. But 714? No way.

As soon as Aaron made his announcement, all of a sudden the press swarmed on him, and the coverage intensified everywhere the team went. I give the Braves a lot of credit in how they handled the madness—especially in 1974 when he broke the record. When Roger Maris hit number 61, there were stories about him losing his hair due to all the stress he was under. I'm not pointing any fingers, but the Yankees didn't really protect him while the media engulfed him. The Braves took a lesson from that, and Donald Davidson, the team's famous traveling secretary and superb public relations guy, was given the responsibility of making sure that there was some kind of sense to the deluge. We couldn't have that crowd around Aaron every day. I never talked to Aaron about it, but he must have appreciated how the team checked him into hotels under an anonymous name. A lot of players do that now, but not many did it then.

To show you the kind of people who got in on the Aaron parade, one guy interviewed Aaron for what seemed like an hour. As he ended the interview, he asked Hank, "By the way, Mr. Aaron, do you hit right-handed or left-handed?" Things like that drove us crazy.

As his pursuit of the record continued, the hate mail poured in. As big a story as the hate mail eventually became, those of us even with the club every day didn't know about it until the end of the

1973 season when Tom Brokaw came to town to do a feature on Aaron. I don't remember all of the documentary he did, but 90 percent of it must have been about the hate mail. The attention only caused more hate mail to come in. I've heard that Aaron still has a lot of that mail. To his credit, he never made it a part of the Ruth chase and handled everything very well.

Aaron's defining moment came when he broke the record, stepped up to the microphone, and said, "I just thank God it's over with." It definitely took a toll on him. I don't think there was any doubt about it.

I was glad that it was over, too, because I had been fretting about having to broadcast the home run. After Aaron reached 700, I went to the Braves and said, "I've been announcing all these years, and I would like to have the privilege of doing the rest of the home runs leading up to 715." Either I was convincing in my argument or they thought it was worthwhile, because they agreed. So every time Aaron batted after that, I did the play-by-play. With Ernie Johnson as my partner, I was doing everything but the third and seventh innings, so a lot of those home runs came in my innings anyway. When 715 came, it had already been established that I was doing it. And it became academic, because it was in the fourth inning and that was one of my innings anyway.

Still, some people thought the move was selfish on my part. Maybe Ernie had some qualms about that. But he never said anything to me. Later on, when I went into the Hall of Fame, some writers tried to get him to talk about it, but his quote at the time was, "I've got no problem with him. He was the No. 1 announcer. It did surprise me a little that he wanted to do it." That was the end of it.

George Plimpton, the famous writer who covered the event, had attempted for some time to get me to tell him how I was going to call the home run. I said, "George, I can't do that. If there's one thing that's my strong suit, it's spontaneity. I can't plan something. I don't want it to sound contrived."

I did give it a lot of thought, though. In my mind, Aaron and Ruth were the same age during their record-setting years and they both hit their record-breaking home runs in Braves uniforms. A lot of people didn't remember that Ruth was a Boston Brave when he hit his last three homers in one game in Pittsburgh, and then retired within two or three days.

So I thought, "When Henry is going to first, I could make some comparison between him and Ruth, then say something else when he was going to second, and so on." Thank God I didn't. I realized I could use that during the time they're getting ready for the ceremony, while they were bringing in his teammates, his parents, his wife Billye, and Bill Bartholomay, the chairman of the board.

Curt Smith, who wrote the book *Voices of the Game*, said my call has stood the test of time. But he wanted to know why.

"The home run dictated what the call was," I said. "The ball barely made it. Aaron did not hit Ruthian home runs. [Bill] Buckner leaped at the old wire fence in left and didn't miss getting it by much. So it wasn't one of those where you could milk it and make it sound spectacular."

The only conscious thing that I did that night was to avoid saying my trademark "Holy Toledo." It was not my moment—it was Hank's.

There was plenty of drama leading up to No. 715. When the '74 season opened in Cincinnati, Aaron played on Opening Day against the Reds at Riverfront Stadium and hit No. 714 off Jack Billingham in the first inning. That tied Ruth's record. Our ballclub wanted to save the record-breaker for the Atlanta opening night at home on Monday. They were thinking about crowds and wanted him to do it in front of his home fans. Eddie Mathews, Aaron's manager and former teammate, announced he wasn't going to play him the next two games. The team's decision to bench Aaron upset commissioner Bowie Kuhn, who said the championship season was open and teams should play their starting lineup or face suspension. Mathews defied him and left Aaron out of the lineup on Saturday, but then Aaron played on Sunday.

Everybody was hoping he wouldn't hit the record-breaker on the road. On Sunday, he took a half swing, with one hand, and the ball almost went out. I don't mean that he was doing it on purpose, but it turned out all right for everybody because that set the stage for Monday night at home against Los Angeles, on national television. Curt Gowdy was there for NBC, and Vin Scully was the Dodger announcer. There was a sellout crowd.

Every show business person came, from Sammy Davis to Pearl Bailey, and they had Jimmy Carter, then the governor, and Atlanta mayor Maynard Jackson in attendance, too. Conspicuous by his absence was Kuhn, who had a prior engagement: he was going to speak to the Cleveland Indians' boosters, the Wahoo Club. The fact remains that with that big of an event, and with him being the commissioner, he should have been there, and I said so on the air. Instead, Kuhn sent Monte Irvin, a good substitute, but it wasn't like having the commissioner there.

With or without the commissioner, I was on the field doing the pregame ceremony. I didn't have much time to think about what I was going to say during the pregame. I did the six o'clock sports on WSB Channel 2, sped to the ballpark, filled out my lineup card, did the pregame show on the radio, and then did the pregame ceremony.

So I truly didn't know what I was going to say if Aaron connected. I had already dedicated myself to the proposition that the home run call wasn't going to sound contrived. Here it is:

"Now here's Henry Aaron. This crowd is up all around. The pitch to him ... bounced it up there, ball one. [Loud round of boos from the audience.] Henry Aaron in the second inning walked and scored. He's sitting on 714. Here's the pitch by Downing . . . swinging ... there's a drive into left-center field. That ball is gonna beeeee ... OUTTA HERE! IT'S GONE! IT'S 715! There's a new home run champion of all time! And it's Henry Aaron! The fireworks are going! Henry Aaron is coming around third! His teammates are at home plate. Listen to this crowd ... [Thunderous sustained applause and cheers from the crowd.]"

After that day, every time I saw Al Downing, who surrendered the record-breaking home run, I said, "You know, Al, you and I are joined at the hip. You threw it and I talked about it."

Over the years, there were a couple of bumps in the road between Henry and me. In my early years in Atlanta, there was a Braves 400 Club luncheon when visiting teams came in. The

Milo emcees the on-the-field festivities to congratulate Hank Aaron for surpassing Babe Ruth's career home run record on April 8, 1974.

Pirates came to town, so they invited Danny Murtaugh, the manager; Bob Prince, the broadcaster; and Roberto Clemente, the star player. The three of them were on the dais—a pretty nice dais for a booster luncheon. I was the emcee for the event.

The year before this luncheon at the All-Star game, Aaron, Mays, and Clemente were the starting outfielders. But because Clemente and Aaron were both right fielders, Walter Alston asked Aaron if he would play left. So at the luncheon, I said that for that All-Star game, Clemente was the right fielder. I didn't say he was the greatest right fielder, or that he had forced Aaron to move to left (the manager did that). Unbeknownst to me, Wilt Browning, the beat writer for the *Atlanta Journal*, went from that luncheon to the ballpark and told Aaron that I had introduced Clemente as the greatest right fielder. It was simply not true.

If Aaron would have asked me about it directly, I could have straightened things out. If necessary, I'd have brought Prince and Murtaugh over there and said, "Will you tell him what I said?" By that time, it was too late for me to address it with Aaron, and Browning had written a story. Thankfully, Donald Davidson, a very close confidant of Aaron, told Henry, "You know he didn't say that." Davidson got us together, and it was a closed issue. And that was the end of it.

Sometime later I was broadcasting a Braves game in Atlanta Stadium, and a ball was hit to Aaron in right field. As he came to field the ball, he juggled it. When he went to pick it up, he dropped it again. Then in his anxiety to throw to second base, he threw it over second baseman Felix Millan's head. Wilt Browning was the official scorer and he gave Millan an error. I didn't agree with the decision and said so on the air.

To me, official scoring is common sense. If it ought to be ruled a hit and the scorer calls it an error, the hitter is unfairly penalized. Common sense should dictate those decisions. In this case, I said, "You know, if you want to really be candid about this play, Aaron could have been given three errors."

When Aaron returned home after the game, his wife had heard about my comments and shared them with Hank. I'm not quite sure what she heard, but she really built it up that I had criticized him roundly. And actually, I was complaining as much about the official scorer as I was criticizing Aaron. Hank said to me, "I thought the broadcaster was supposed to favor the home players." It became a bigger story than my supposed comments at the luncheon; the story was even picked up by the *Chicago Tribune*. Some friends from Chicago called and said, "What the hell are you doing down there?" A couple days later, Donald Davidson once again got Aaron and me together in his suite at the hotel, and we ironed things out.

To Aaron's credit, when I went into the Hall of Fame in 1992, the writer who covered the event for the Atlanta newspaper wrote some nice things about me, but also wanted to include the controversies between Aaron and me. Hank skirted talking about any previous incidents—saying that neither of us even mentioned it anymore—and had only positive things to say about me: "I respect Milo. I have great memories of being with him. . . . I can honestly say that I don't think any announcer around has the voice, and does the work, and can announce the games as well as Milo, and I think he deserves to be in the Hall of Fame."

Does that sound like a guy who held a grudge against me? If Aaron hadn't handled it in that dignified manner, our controversies of old would have become a story again just at the time I was going into the Baseball Hall of Fame. I've been forever grateful to him and told him that when I saw him later.

The truth about Aaron is that he was somewhat overlooked—especially in his younger years. He was a superstar for certain, but he was also shy and withdrawn—a quiet and easygoing guy. He didn't get the publicity he deserved. The press drooled over Willie Mays, Mickey Mantle, and Duke Snider, three of the greatest outfielders of their time playing within two miles of each other in New York City. But where was the attention due to Aaron, who was putting up one terrific season after another in Milwaukee? Hank was also overshadowed by his teammates—Eddie Mathews, Joe Adcock, and Warren Spahn. And later Phil Niekro and Rico Carty. While Niekro was not all that outgoing, he was a media favorite.

Thirty-plus years later, I still don't see Aaron on T.V. commercials. I hear them talk about a lot of the old players, but I don't think they include Aaron in their conversations enough of the time. I've said it on the air, and I've said it in speaking engagements: he should have gotten more credit.

Aaron performed pretty much without the glare of the publicity spotlight—until he was closing in on the home run record. And that lack of media pressure might have helped him out some. Eddie Mathews and Joe Adcock definitely helped out, with each providing protection in the lineup for the other two. Mathews, of course, was a Hall of Fame slugger, and the only man to play for the same club in three different cities: Boston, Milwaukee, and Atlanta. Aaron and Mathews showed a great deal of respect for each other. And they had a lot of success together. Very few people realize they hold the record for most home runs by a pair of teammates (863). That respect carried over to when Mathews was Aaron's manager. Mathews stuck his neck out to bench Aaron after he hit home run No. 714 so that Aaron could hit No. 715 at home.

Henry was usually a pretty quiet and easygoing guy. But there were exceptions. In 1972 he got into a fight with teammate Rico Carty on an airplane. Carty resented Aaron—possibly there was some jealousy at play as they were both elite hitters. The two of them had a mutual dislike for each other, and on this plane trip it boiled over. The fight started as a disagreement over word choice.

Carty was Dominican, not African-American. So he didn't think he was black, and he didn't like to be thought of as black. In this instance, Carty called Aaron "a black son-of-a-bitch" and Aaron replied, "You're not exactly pink yourself."

I once heard Rico make a comment to Lou Brock around the batting cage. Carty said to Brock, "Man, you're so black, you're blue." But Brock didn't say anything in response. He knew Carty was jacking around and there wasn't anything to it. But when Carty and Aaron said it to each other, it was another case altogether—things just exploded. Carty was a boxer as a kid—until he got knocked out and his mother made him quit. But he took care of Aaron with one punch. I was there—the fight happened right next to me.

If such a fight were to happen today, the mass media would have been all over it. Fortunately it happened in the early '70s, and it never really became a story. Plus the Braves didn't let those kind of incidents get out of hand. Cooler heads prevailed. They traded Rico to the Texas Rangers. The incident was over, and that was the end of it.

The first Opening Day pitcher in Atlanta's history was Tony Cloninger. Tony was a southern boy from North Carolina, and he was so excited to pitch that opening game, the first major league game to be played in the South. He was pitching against Bob Veale,

Milo greets the baseball fans of Atlanta in 1966 during an Opening Day motorcade.

a power pitcher with the Pittsburgh Pirates. Joe Torre hit two home runs in that game—but Tony Cloninger was the real story.

In the first game of the season, Cloninger, who threw a heavy sinker that was like a shotput, pitched a complete game. That in and of itself wasn't a huge feat; what made it spectacular was the game went 13 innings! He didn't want to come out of the game, and he probably hurt his arm as a result. Pitching in front of his relatives and his friends, Tony's pride kicked in. He'd won 24 games the year before in Milwaukee, but he was never the same after that first game in Atlanta. Worst of all—he lost, 3-2, after surrendering two runs in the top of the 13th inning.

His pitching wasn't the same after that start, but he had no problems at the plate. In 1966, he hit five home runs, five doubles, and drove in 23 RBI. I'll never forget what he did on July 3, 1966. We were playing at Candlestick Park in San Francisco. He hit a grand slam in the first inning and another one in the fourth inning. That made him the first National League *player* to hit two grand slams in one game. He got a ninth RBI during the same game with a single. We won, 17–3, and Tony again went the distance on the mound.

Although Cloninger burned out quickly, Niekro soon replaced him as the ace of the staff. For the most part, Niekro just did his thing. He spent a lot of time in the trainer's room, but if you needed him, he was accessible and had a great sense of humor. And he wrote a lot of poetry, which was unique for a ball player.

The joke about Niekro was that as soon as the bus driver started the engine, Niekro would be asleep. I never saw a guy who could go to sleep like that. It was like he snapped his fingers and it was good night. He was a very relaxed guy, to say the least.

I remember his first start of the 1967 season—and only his second career start—very well. Niekro began the year working out of the bullpen as the closer, but in a series against Philadelphia, Braves skipper Billy Hitchcock needed an emergency starter and called upon Niekro. He was simply amazing that game, giving up just two hits, three walks, and no runs in a complete-game victory.

The guy who really helped Niekro was Bob Uecker, the good-field, no-hit catcher who backed up Joe Torre for part of the 1967 season. Uecker's famous line about Niekro the knuckleballer was, "How do you catch Phil Niekro? You let the ball go, and when it stops rolling, you pick it up."

A couple of years later, Niekro got even more help behind the plate from Bob Didier, a rookie on the '69 team who could really catch that knuckleball. The Braves won the West that year and played the Mets for the right to go to the World Series. Niekro made a strong case for the Cy Young award that season. He had two sure wins rained out but still won 23 games and posted 21 complete games with a 2.56 ERA.

When the knuckler was working, Niekro was unhittable. He proved that in 1973, when he threw his only no-hitter against the Padres. Usually, a knuckleball pitcher will be forced to throw a fastball or two if he gets behind in the count, and then somebody's going to get a hit. But nobody did that day, and the knuckler was dancing all over the place. He wound up walking three to spoil a perfect game, but we won, 9–0.

In contrast to Phil's no-hitter, Cubs hurler Kenny Holtzman pitched a no-hitter against the Braves on August 19, 1969, and didn't strike out anybody. That was the only time that ever happened. After that game, which found Atlanta two and a half games out and in a five-team divisional race, the Braves got hot and finished strong, winning the division by three games over the Giants.

The guy who really came to the forefront on that '69 pitching staff was Ron Reed. They made a starter out of him, and he won 18 games. Hoyt Wilhelm helped in September, too. He was acquired from the Angels, but he didn't join the club in time to qualify for the playoffs. If the Braves would have had Wilhelm for those playoff games with the Mets, they might have been in the World Series instead of the Amazin' Mets.

With the '69 Braves, I was able to see the two greatest knuckleball pitchers of all time on the same club in Niekro and Wilhelm. Paul Richards, one of my favorite people of all time in the game and the Atlanta general manager then, was the guy who designed the big catcher's mitt while with Baltimore so that somebody could actually catch Wilhelm's knuckler.

The Atlanta broadcast booth, at least in those early years, had all the ups and downs of a knuckleball. We had three announcers, but only two of them worked together. Ernie Johnson was there, but he was the assistant director of broadcasting and only announced when we televised games, which we rarely did during those first two or three years. Larry Munson was the third guy, but he only lasted two years with us before becoming an outstanding football announcer for the Georgia Bulldogs. When the games were televised, I did the bulk of the television. Ernie Johnson was with me on TV, and Munson worked radio alone.

After the first couple of years, it became evident that Munson, if he knew anything about baseball, didn't display it. That was a shock, because he'd done 13 years of minor-league baseball in

Nashville before joining us. He brought nothing to the table. He seemed to think that if you showed up with a pencil and a scorecard, that was your preparation.

In contrast, I enjoyed what Ernie Johnson was doing with me on TV. And I was gung-ho to have a former player with me and utilize him as an analyst, maybe having him do an inning or two. I didn't think anybody ought to do all nine innings; each announcer deserved a breather, as did the listener.

After two years of working with Munson, I was fed up. I went to the ballclub and said, "Ernie Johnson is doing a great job. I'd like to have it turned into a two-man team and I'd like to have Ernie become the full-time analyst and do the third and the seventh innings." The club agreed, and Ernie became a very good sidekick. I liked Ernie both on and off the air.

But that doesn't mean that we always saw eye to eye. I recall one game that I broadcast when Phil Niekro was on the mound for a Sunday afternoon game in Atlanta Stadium. The ballclub was enjoying a nice win streak, but only 4,000 people showed up at the game. On the air I commented about the poor attendance: "You know, some people have been saying that the reason they haven't been coming to the games lately is because the team isn't winning. Well, they're winning now. And one of your favorite players, Phil Niekro, is pitching this game. That begs the question: why is our attendance only 4,000?"

The next day, The *Journal-Constitution* wrote about my comment on attendance and took it way out of context. They said I was blaming the fans and criticizing them for not coming to the games. And that wasn't why I said it. If Phil Niekro was pitching a Sunday game and Henry Aaron was on the club, along with all those other stars, I felt it was fair to question why the attendance was so poor in a town of two or three million. The Atlanta Crackers drew more than that when they were in Double-A and Triple-A.

Ernie Johnson was then director of broadcasting, and he jumped my bones about my comment. I wouldn't say that we became embroiled in a lengthy argument, but I took offense that he thought it was important to bounce me on it.

Ted Turner purchased the Braves franchise in 1976. And that's when Ernie Johnson struck a second time. Before the sale of the team, he went to the ballclub and said, "I'll do the games for the same salary you're paying me to be the director of broadcasting." And the team bought it, thinking that having Johnson on board at a lesser amount than I was making would make the sale more attractive to billionaire Ted Turner. So they decided not to renew my contract, and once again I was looking for work.

Turner liked me as an announcer—as I soon found out in public. I went to the Braves 400 annual banquet in 1976 even though I already had a job with another franchise. Turner got up to speak at the banquet as the new owner. He looked out in the large crowd, saw me, and said, "If I'd have bought this ballclub a month sooner, Milo Hamilton would still be the broadcaster." Later on, I asked, "Did somebody here really think that my salary was going to deter Turner from buying the club?"

I had spent 10 years in Atlanta and seen some historic things, but I knew it was time to move on. I was aware that the Cardinal job was going to be open because Jack Buck was going to be offered a television job in New York for a show called *Grandstand*. The Cardinals asked for and received permission from the Braves to talk to me about their opening. I went for the interview and the owners (Anheuser-Busch), the Cardinals, and KMOX all liked me. They offered me a two-year deal, and I was ready to sign it. A few more days went by, and we were waiting for approval from Mike Riorty, a top sports executive with the brewery.

I finally called my friend, Dolan Walsh, who was familiar with my negotiations with the team and worked for a firm that was employed by the Cardinals. Dolan was one of my big boosters because he was the person who had hired me to do Cardinal games way back in 1954. I asked Dolan, "When do you think we're going to sign this thing?" And he said, "Any day, I think. It's all done." A few more days passed and Dolan finally got antsy about it and called Riorty himself. Mike asked him, "Can you meet me for a drink at five o'clock?" The two met. They were sitting across the table looking at each other, and Mike said to Dolan, "What if

Grandstand fails?" Dolan read that perfectly. It meant that the team had promised Buck he could come back if need be.

The safety valve for them was Bob Star, who had been on the broadcast crew with Buck and Mike Shannon. They figured they could give the job to Star, a fine broadcaster. In a way, they kind of took advantage of him because they figured they could promote him, and if Buck came back, they would then demote him. They knew I wasn't going to come for a year and take a chance and uproot my family. Their hunch was right: *Grandstand* didn't work out, and Buck was soon back with the Cards. By his own admission, it was the biggest mistake Buck ever made.

The downside for me was that I wasn't going back to St. Louis. Instead, I was headed to Pittsburgh.

9

NO PRINCE IN PITTSBURGH

It was impossible to replace Bob Prince as Voice of the Pirates. I wasn't a carouser, which Prince was, and so I didn't go out drinking every night with the writers like he did. That's the way he lived. He never got anybody into trouble, but Prince had been warned that if he didn't clean up his act, he was going to lose his job. And that's exactly what happened.

When I got the job after the 1975 season, I went to a baseball dinner and Prince was there and said, "Well, kid, you'll only be here a year." I said, "Bob, I bought a condominium here. I've got a four-year contract." He blanched. He had no idea.

Prince continued to make appearances around town. He would get a snoot-full someplace, and he'd start spouting off about the team or the way he was treated, or worse yet, me. Remember: he got fired. I didn't take his job. I just happened to be the guy they hired to replace him. But Prince wouldn't let up. He was telling everyone, "I'm going to be back next year."

The Pittsburgh fans were great to me, though. Even when I go back to Pittsburgh now, a lot of the fans still remember me and will say, "Boy, we loved you when you were here." And the players were great to me as well. In fact, Willie Stargell had been a big friend of Prince's but still welcomed me on board. When I accompanied the team on its first caravan before the 1976 season, Stargell said to me, "You're the new broadcaster. I respect that. I was a great friend of Prince's, but as far as I'm concerned, you're the Pirate broadcaster now." And he treated me great for four years.

The only guy who really resented me—and I think it was a pride thing—was pitcher Bruce Kison. He never said anything to me, but I didn't fall off a turnip truck. I was good at reading guys, and I could tell that he didn't care for me. He had named his first son after Bob Prince, so he obviously truly liked the man. But after my first year in Pittsburgh, Kison took the chip off his shoulder and accepted me.

I t took several years for the Pirates to build their world championship club of 1979. In 1976, my first year with the team, we finished second, nine games behind Philadelphia, under Danny Murtaugh, in his fourth term at the helm. But he passed away after the season, so we brought in new manager Chuck Tanner. We got Tanner, a very good manager, in an unusual way: the Pirates traded Manny Sanguillen, their No. 1 catcher, to Oakland for Chuck Tanner and a good chunk of cash. Charlie Finley, the owner of the A's, had insisted on getting a good player if he was going to release Tanner from his contract.

Tanner was an effervescent presence in the dugout, and his personality carried over off the field, too. I used to go to his office after almost every game because we really had a great relationship, and I loved to hear him talk. We knew each other prior to his arrival in Pittsburgh because I had broadcast his games when he came up with the Milwaukee Braves as an outfielder in the mid

'50s. He hit a home run in his first at-bat. Unfortunately, an Achilles injury cut his career short.

Tanner's optimism was contagious, but it was also so overwhelming at times that a lot of people thought it was an act. People finally realized that with Chuck Tanner, what you see is what you get. That's the way he lived his life with his family, with his friends, on the golf course, out to dinner, at the ballpark, anywhere. He's not trying to BS you. That's just the way he is.

Tanner had great rapport with the writers. Somebody would say, "Joe Jones has really been playing great for the last five days. Why don't you play him all the time instead of letting him sit on the bench?" And Chuck would look right back at the writer and he'd say, "because the ball will find him," which would get a good chuckle from the press. "He's a bench guy for a reason. He'll fill in for you and do a good job for you, but he's not an everyday player."

Tanner was great with his players. If he ever admonished any of them, I never knew about it. It never made its way into the paper. He loved his players, and he was careful not to embarrass them.

Trading for Tanner worked out well on the field as well as in the clubhouse. We were only five games out in 1977 and a game and a half behind in 1978, finishing second to the Phillies both years. In the dugout, Tanner didn't play by the book all the time; instead, he often managed using his gut instinct. But Tanner's magic wouldn't have worked without a strong team on the field.

While in Oakland, Tanner had Phil Garner at second base, and he wanted him badly in Pittsburgh. So we brought him over in spring training of 1977 in a nine-player trade. The Pirates already had a second baseman, Rennie Stennett, so they moved Garner to third. He did a good job for us, and he stole a lot of bases, which was to Tanner's liking. Under Tanner, even if a player couldn't run, he still stole bases. Tanner taught Garner—just as he did others— that you don't steal bases with your speed, you do it with your inclinations and by reading pitchers. We had eight guys steal over 10 bases that year, and believe me, some of them—like Dave Parker—didn't look like typical base-stealers.

In August of 1978, we were eight and a half games back of Philadelphia and in fourth place, heading to Veteran's Stadium for a big series with the first-place Phillies. We dropped the series, losing three out of four, to fall to 10½ games back. The writers came out with their black paint brushes in hand, asking, "Well, Chuck, is it over?" Tanner replied, "I don't think so. What day is this?"

Sure enough, Tanner got the guys on track, and over the final two months of the season we put together winning streaks of 11, 10, and seven games to get back into the race. We weren't knocked out until the next-to-last game of the season. We trailed the Phillies by one and a half games with just two games left. Our opponent? The Phillies.

In that deciding game, Stargell hit a grand slam in the first inning. We got a lead of 4-1 and said, "Here we go now!" But then Randy Lersch, their pitcher, hit a pair of home runs to spark their offense to a 10-4 lead heading into the bottom of the ninth. With a comfortable six-run lead, Tug McGraw couldn't get anyone out, and we came storming back for four runs. But Ron Reed bailed out McGraw before we could tie it up, and we were officially eliminated.

If we had listened to the beat writers instead of Chuck Tanner after the game after losing that series to the Phillies in the middle of August, the race for the division title would have been over many weeks earlier. But Tanner wouldn't let the club quit—and that momentum continued on into 1979.

But first, we had to make some personnel changes. Frank Taveras, our Opening Day shortstop, made a bad error in the first inning of a game early in April. He came back into the dugout and gave Tanner the excuse that he was sick. That was all Tanner could take. He went to general manager Pete Peterson and said, "You've got to get me a shortstop."

The Pirates traded for Mets shortstop Tim Foli, which worked out great for two reasons. First, Foli was a great defensive shortstop. A lot of managers today like a "two-out shortstop." If the game is on the line they need a big out, and managers want the ball hit to their shortstop so he can make the big play, whether it's tough or simply routine. Foli was that kind of a player. Plus he was the perfect No. 2 hitter. With Taveras out of the leadoff slot, Omar

The first—and only—time I've celebrated a World Series championship came in 1979 with Pittsburgh. Here, Omar Moreno and teammates celebrate on the field.
Focus on Sport/Getty Images

Moreno moved from the two-hole to leadoff and became a great base-stealing threat at the top of our order.

Foli knew when to take a pitch, and he knew how to fake the bunt and distract the catcher. Longtime Astros catcher Alan Ashby told me on many occasions that he hated to catch with Foli at the plate. More so than anybody else, Foli would do anything to bother the pitcher and the catcher. It gave the baserunner an extra step or two in his lead and helped Moreno steal 77 bases that year.

The Pirates also traded for third baseman Bill Madlock in June, which enabled Garner to go back to his regular spot at second. Now they had a complete ballclub: Stargell, Garner, Foli, Madlock, Bill Robinson, Moreno, and Parker. And a club that wasn't picked to make much noise won the division on the last day of the season and then came storming back from a three-games-to-one deficit against Baltimore to take the World Championship.

Winning the 1979 World Series was definitely the highlight of my time in Pittsburgh. But the ring didn't come easy. In Game 4 of the series, we blew a 6-3 lead in the eighth when Don Robinson and Kent Tekulve, our closer, got shellacked. In a desperation start the next day, Jim Rooker, a journeyman lefty who hadn't had a good season, pitched the game of his life. After that 7-1 win, we were still down, three games to two, and had to go to Baltimore for the sixth and seventh games. We beat them 4-0 and 4-1 to win it all.

Talk about pandemonium in the clubhouse! There's nothing like a World Series-winning clubhouse. Whew! I got soaked with champagne. But the championship celebration was somewhat bittersweet, as by the time the World Series ended, I already knew that I was going to work in Chicago the following year.

We had a big parade in New Castle, Pennsylvania, Tanner's hometown, about an hour from Pittsburgh. There were 50,000 people at the parade, including some of the team's owners. I introduced Tanner as the lead speaker in front of all of his friends. As I introduced him, I said, "This will be the last time I introduce Chuck Tanner." And he didn't quite know what to think. But after his speech, I told him that I was leaving to become Jack Brickhouse's successor with the Cubs.

As luck would have it, the Pirates opened the 1980 season against the Cubs in Pittsburgh. The Pirates were handing out the World Series rings before the game. Even though I had resigned, Pete Peterson called me in and said, "Come over. We've got to measure you for your World Series ring." They gave out the rings at home plate, and I got mine on national TV (WGN) along with the rest of the Pirates. That meant a lot to me.

10

CAGED BY THE CANARY

My return to Chicago actually began during spring training in 1979. My wife, Arlene, and I were having dinner at the Columbia restaurant at St. Armands Circle in Sarasota, Florida, right down the road from Bradenton, where the Pittsburgh Pirates trained. At the time, I was starting the fourth year of my radio contract covering the Pirates for KDKA, and I mentioned to Arlene that night that I had decided it was time to leave that job. I didn't know where I would be in 1980, but it wasn't going to be Pittsburgh. I had to find another job. I loved the city of Pittsburgh and enjoyed my relationship with the players, organization, and station. But there was no way I could continue to prove to the media that I was good enough to replace the legendary Bob Prince. It was a no-win situation for me.

Fate stepped in again. Midway through the 1979 season, I got a call from the brass at WGN in Chicago. They thought Jack

Brickhouse was slipping a bit with his voice, and the work schedule was taking its toll on a fellow approaching age 65. In those days, 65 was an age where a lot of companies sent you out the door with a gold watch and a going-away party.

WGN huddled with Jack and agreed to let him work the 1980 season and then bring me aboard in 1981. When Brickhouse came to Pittsburgh in the summer of '79, he and I dined at Poli's. When the Pirates went into Chicago a few weeks later, WGN had arranged to have me audition on television—unbeknownst to me—with Lou Boudreau during a pregame show. It was set up so that I would talk about the Pirates and our World Series chances. But that interview also served—as I found out later—as an opportunity for the WGN brass to see me in action, to check my on-camera presence.

I guess I didn't scare anyone, because a couple of days after the Pirates' victory parade, I went to Chicago and signed my WGN contract. Jack said he was very happy about my selection and especially pleased that WGN had given him the opportunity to pick his successor. Jack congratulated Arlene on my new job over the phone, and I remember Arlene telling Jack, "I guess I better call the moving van." To which Jack replied, "But Arlene, isn't it nice to know you'll never have to call one again?" In other words, Brickhouse was telling her that WGN was going to let me work the rest of my life at the station, doing Chicago Cubs baseball. It's pretty hard to forget that kind of a quote.

A week later, Gary Deeb, the often-controversial radio and TV critic who wrote for *The Chicago Tribune* (and later *The Sun-Times* and WLS-TV), wrote a story about my hiring with a headline the size of the Pearl Harbor bombing announcement. It was huge and was positioned on the front page of the sports section. It couldn't have been a more flattering article if I had written it myself. The article discussed my loyal following from my days with the White Sox and my DJ show. Deeb mentioned in the article that Brickhouse had been allowed by the folks at WGN to choose me as his successor. He wrote all the right things for all the right people.

Milo in the WGN booth in Chicago, 1980.

All that was left to do after the big hurrah over my hiring was to get to work. It was decided by WGN management and Brickhouse that I would work alongside Jack during the 1980 baseball season, and then take over as the lead play-by-play announcer in 1981. Jack was fine with that and so was I. It looked like things would go smoothly. The 1980 season got underway and everything was beautiful. Preston Gomez started out as Cubs manager, and Bob Kennedy was the GM. But the Cubs weren't a good team that year, and after getting off slowly, Gomez was replaced by Joey Amalfitano. Despite a new leader, the team continued to perform poorly, and we finished the '80 season in last place. But Jack and I had a good run of it in the booth.

When fall came around, WGN asked me to step in and do some basketball on television. So I did DePaul and Chicago Bulls games. That was great because I loved doing basketball. It was a nice change of pace and it was good for WGN to have me on the air all year long. So there I was, moving right along, doing basketball during the winter and preparing for the start of spring training in Arizona in a few months.

Then, sometime during that winter, I guess it dawned on Brickhouse that he really *was* retired. That hit him hard. He called WGN and asked if he could hang around a little longer, perhaps the first half of the 1981 season, and then hand me the reins. I was okay with that, because I pretty much knew that the final decision on Jack's last day would always be Jack's to make. Who was I to say anything that could be construed as being negative? This was Jack Brickhouse, a Chicago legend, a man who had been very good to my family and me. If Jack needed a little more time in the booth, I had no problem with that.

1981 was a turbulent season for baseball in Chicago. It was the year of the player strike, and also the year young Bill Wrigley decided to sell the franchise to the Tribune Company. The player strike began in June and went beyond the All-Star break before it was settled. Meanwhile, it was decided by WGN that Brickhouse would turn over the lead role to me for the first game after the strike. Jack did turn over the reins, but he also decided to hang

Legendary Cubs broadcaster Jack Brickhouse poses with Milo in 1979.

around the rest of the season as my sidekick in the booth, which was just fine with me.

When I started at WGN during the 1980 season, I did the third, fourth, and eighth innings. Now Jack and I reversed that: I handled the first, second, fifth, sixth, and ninth innings, and he did three, four, and eight. The 1981 season finally concluded, and we had a nice going-away party for Jack at the old Press Club inside the Wrigley Building. At that event, Jack was having fun, and it wasn't long before he called me over with a familiar request: "Tell some Bob Elson stories."

I thought, "Gosh, Jack, this ain't the place to tell Elson stories." But he begged me, so I went ahead and told some Elson stories and did some impersonations for the crowd that had gathered.

One of my favorite impersonations follows: "Ya know, the Whiiiite Sox are opening a BIG weekend series with the New York Yankees. We'll be playing them on Friday night, Saturday afternoon, and a big Sunday doubleheader. Yankees manager Casey Stengel told me that Allie Reynolds will pitch on Friday night, Saturday afternoon it'll be Vic Raschi, and on Sunday afternoon in the first game it'll be Whitey Ford. And he told me he'd tell me at dinner on Thursday night at Fritzell's who's gonna pitch the second game. And you know, you'll be able to get your tickets, you can get them downtown, and we want you to be at all of those games cause it's a big, big series with the New York Yankees . . . that's a ball, a strike, and another ball."

One of the people in attendance at the party was Tribune Company CEO Stanton Cook, a gracious executive with silver hair and a look of class. "I've never heard you do those Elson impersonations," Cook told me, laughing. "You sound *exactly* like Bob Elson." Stanton had grown up listening to Elson, and I guess he had never heard me do my take. After all, I hadn't been around him in that kind of an atmosphere before.

Not long after the Brickhouse party, I got a telephone call at nine o'clock in the morning from Sheldon Cooper, one of the vice presidents at the TV station. He told me to head over to the Ambassador Hotel because there would be an important announcement later that morning. I pressed him a bit to explain

but Cooper bluntly told me they *needed* me there without explaining why. "We really need you there," he repeated before hanging up. I had no clue what was in store for me that day.

I arrived at the hotel and found the room where the press conference was being held. Moments later, to my complete surprise, it was announced that Harry Caray was going to be the lead TV announcer for the Chicago Cubs. My heart lept into my throat.

Caray had been with the White Sox for a number of years throughout the 1970s, teaming with Jimmy Piersall until they had a falling out with team owners Eddie Einhorn and Jerry Reinsdorf. Quite honestly, I didn't handle myself well during the announcement. There I was, standing completely by myself at the back of the room, watching this goddamn thing unfold in front of me. I realized that I had been thrown a wicked curve.

After the announcement, Brickhouse came over, the hurt written across his face, and said softly, "I tried to talk them out of it, Milo. I told Jim Dowdle he owes you better than that." Then Andy McKenna, who owned a local paper company and was on the Cubs' board of directors, wandered over to me. "Can we have lunch tomorrow?" he asked. After I agreed, he said, "You know Stan Cook was not in favor of this move. Mrs. Cook especially was not in favor of it. She didn't think anybody like Caray should ever work for *The Tribune*. She feels it's not in their image."

McKenna went on to say that he had also told Dowdle that hiring Caray was the wrong move, but he met resistance. At least McKenna took me to lunch and explained that others had fought against the hiring of Caray, but that Dowdle had decided he was going to do it regardless. It was going to be Dowdle's footprint on the Cubs. He hadn't been on the *Tribune* board for long, so now he was going to show everybody who was boss. Little did the people at WGN know that this move would trigger other moves. The WGN crew that I was a part of was very popular and a great group of employees, but Dowdle fired most of them, including guys who had been at the station forever. Those cameramen were like a family. He put them on a *per diem* and took away their benefits. It was brutal.

After the Caray announcement, Dowdle soon realized that he was going to have to mend a fence. So he signed me to a new contract to be Caray's broadcasting partner. I swallowed my pride and attempted to put my best foot forward. Dowdle invited Caray and me to meet him for dinner at the Drake Hotel on Michigan Avenue. He wanted to see if he could get us on the same page before the start of spring training. I swallowed my pride once again and agreed to meet them.

I arrived at the Drake and went into the dining room. It was just the three of us at the table. Caray opened the conversation rather straightforwardly, saying, "Well, kid, if I were you, I'd leave town." So much for "How's the family?" and other such pleasantries. Dowdle sensed the tension in the air and stepped right in, saying, "Harry, that's not possible. Milo has a new contract."

Now it was Caray's turn to be surprised. Caray wasn't ready for that news and looked rather upset. Dowdle kept on, trying to mend the fence, and by the end of dinner, we all agreed to act professional toward each other and make it work.

Caray and I got through spring training without any problems as we prepared for the 1982 season under new Cubs manager Lee Elia and general manager Dallas Green. The Cubs had adopted a new theme which they called "Building a New Tradition."

Early that 1982 season, I went out of my way to help Caray escape an awkward situation during one of our broadcasts. It had been a rather cold spring in Chicago and the Cubs had hired a young woman, Marla Collins, to be their ball girl. She would dress up for home games in a Cubs uniform and sit in a small folding chair right behind the on-deck circle along the first-base line. Her job was to bring more baseballs to the home plate umpire and occasionally bring him a cup of water.

On one particular day, with the weather improving and the temperature climbing into the 70s, Marla unveiled a new part of her ballgame attire—specifically "hot pants" to replace the normal baseball pants. We were doing our broadcast, and all of a sudden I hear Caray belt out, "Well, today's the first day we've seen Marla *without* her pants on." Seconds later, Harry realized what he had said, and more importantly how his audience might interpret it. He

got to laughing real hard and this kept on for at least a full minute. It was getting embarrassing so finally I just said, "Harry, it might be a good idea if we went to a commercial."

Needless to say, that "Cubs Moment" made it onto several TV recaps that evening and has been played back countless times over the years on radio, including on Wally Phillips's morning show on WGN. Wally got plenty of good mileage out of that gaffe.

Being around Caray, day after day, was a real challenge. Harry's handling of people was poor to say the least. It didn't matter if he was dealing with the starting pitcher, traveling secretary, the public relations person, or an usher. He didn't let go of mistakes—he dwelled on them. If a player made an error on a Tuesday and it cost the Cubs the game, he rode that error for a week. He rode managers. He rode players. It didn't matter. He treated everyone the same way. In short, he was a miserable human being.

As a result, there were a lot of folks in the media waiting for the fireworks to begin between Caray and me. At the start of spring training, the coast was clear. But I wasn't naive, either. I was still determined to keep our relationship professional and just go about my business. I had something more important to worry about, anyway. Around the start of the '82 season, I discovered that my health wasn't good. During spring training, the doctors informed me that I was close to needing chemotherapy to fight my leukemia. That spring and early summer were a real battle. Even on my good days, I was in lots of pain.

On a trip to St. Louis in early July, I was inside a coffee shop when the pain began to get real bad. I guess all the drugs I had been taking were beginning to take a toll on my system. I ran into one of the Cubs public relations staffers and asked him to locate WGN producer Arne Harris. I knew I had to fly back to Chicago to seek medical help and I needed to tell Arne to get a replacement for me for that night's game. I telephoned my hematologist and he told me to get back right away.

Back in Chicago, I was admitted to Northwestern Memorial Hospital. Not long after, guess who dropped by my hospital room? None other than Jim Dowdle. It was almost as if he was dropping in to see if I was really that ill, if perhaps I was faking it. I could sense that from his body language. Can you imagine anyone being that inconsiderate?

My wife was also there when Dowdle showed up, along with my doctor. Dowdle could see that I had wires and tubes coming out of me everywhere, and my body was covered in heating pads, too. The doctors were doing everything they could to make me feel better. As Dowdle began to leave the room, he looked over at my doctor and said, "Boy, he really is sick, isn't he?" My doctor— who was a big fan of mine and was aware of some of the things that had been going on behind the scenes at that time—looked right at Dowdle and said, "One of the worst things a person battling leukemia can have happen is to be put under enormous stress." Then he paused for emphasis before adding, "And *you're* one of the primary reasons he's lying there!"

Being away from the broadcast booth only made matters worse. To show the insensitive side of "the Canary"—the name Harry picked up while in St. Louis—I was watching the game on TV from the hospital when I heard Caray actually make fun of my medical situation on the broadcast. At one point, he said on the air, "You know, I never missed *any* games. I don't understand how a guy can take time off during the season."

But I didn't take much time off. I made it back into the booth right after the All-Star break. Dowdle had told me to stay out during the break, giving me an extra three days, and then come back. When I returned, the abuse from Caray continued. Not long after my return, we were in Houston for a series and Caray gave a story to a reporter from *The Houston Chronicle*. He was quoted as boasting about "never missing an inning of any game" in his broadcasting career "unlike some other broadcasters I know." That was a direct knock on me and a real cheap shot. It was just another case of "the Canary" rubbing it in. He just never let go.

You can imagine the temptation for me later on, when that sonofabitch suffered a stroke in 1987, to say something bad about him. But I didn't. It's not in my nature. And unlike Caray, I had chosen to let it go. It wasn't until much later that I spoke out.

I was stunned—and saddened—when the Cubs erected a statue of Caray along Addison Street, outside the gate where the visiting teams enter Wrigley Field. The first statue put up outside Wrigley Field *should have been* for Ernie Banks. That's a given. And if the team was going to add any others, they should have considered Billy Williams, Fergie Jenkins, or Ron Santo. It's no real surprise that the Caray statue was a Dowdle idea, too.

If the team was going to erect a statue of a broadcaster outside the park, it should have been Jack Brickhouse. That man was there for 40 years when the team was pitiful, and he was the guy who saved the Cubs' broadcast. Instead, they put him up on a foul pole inside the park, while that statue of "the Canary" went up outside. Due to its location, I see that statue every time the Astros visit Wrigley Field as our bus pulls up to the park. When I get off the bus, I say to myself, "I gotta go get some peanuts and feed the pigeons so they'll fly over the statue all day long."

Getting back to the 1982 season, somehow Caray and I eventually got through the year. As we were closing off the final telecast on Channel 9, I turned to Caray and said, "Harry, we made it through the season . . . and how many people thought we'd be able to do that?" He got a chuckle out of that one.

At the season's end, WGN let it be known that they wanted Vince Lloyd out of the radio booth. So the brass came to me. I had let my feelings be known that I would really love to do radio almost exclusively if the opportunity ever presented itself. WGN thought the time was right to move me over to the radio side, with Lou Boudreau as my partner, so it was agreed that I would be the lead radio broadcaster during the 1983 season. Working with Lou instead of Harry was a night and day difference. Lou was great to me. The year I was on chemotherapy, Lou checked up on me *every* day. I will never forget that kind of compassion, especially when Caray was treating me like a cur dog. Boudreau kept my spirits going.

I tried to give Lou more of an opportunity to talk baseball because he was just so good at it. I also felt that the analyst should play a more important role in the broadcast than the play-by-play person. Lou made that an easy decision because he was a baseball encyclopedia. I always enjoyed our dinners on road trips because I learned so much about baseball from listening to him. Some of the analysts today think they have to be slick, but Lou just talked baseball, which was enough. That's what made "Good Kid"—as he was called—so charming. He wasn't polished, and his style might not have worked in a city other than Chicago, where he'd been a standout athlete in high school and later at the University of Illinois before starting his Hall of Fame career with Cleveland. Lou was an icon, so his audience accepted Lou for what he was.

The 1983 season was also the first for Steve Stone, the former Cy Young Award winner with the Orioles. He became Caray's new partner on the TV side while Vince Lloyd teamed with producer Jack Rosenberg to start up the new Cubs radio network, something they turned into a tremendous success. Vince would still hang around with Lou and me in the radio booth at home games and during a few road contests, to inject a comment here and there, but he was pretty much left out of the broadcast picture.

Caray still felt like he had to stick his nose into the radio booth, so during the middle three innings of our broadcasts, he came over to the radio side with Lou, and I went over to the television booth with Steve. That was always an interesting trip as we passed each other on the catwalk outside the two booths. Caray and I wouldn't even acknowledge each other on most days.

Even after I had left TV to become Lou's partner on the radio, Caray continued to annoy me on so many levels—not the least of which was his approach to singing "Take Me Out to the Ballgame" during the seventh-inning stretch. He would get up to sing in the TV booth and I would immediately walk out the back door of the radio booth and stand silently on the catwalk, facing the fans in the lower stands below. It was my silent protest, I suppose. I didn't want to be any part of his act, and it was a stand I took for all the years of being treated so shabbily by that man. It wasn't in me to stand up and be part of his act.

On occasion, I wasn't too shy to tell him what I thought, either. "Harry," I once said, "the people down there in the stands didn't come here to hear you sing or watch you sing." And he said to me, "Whaddya mean?" I replied, "Let's do this. Suppose next Thursday is an open date and there's no game here at Wrigley Field. Let's announce in the papers that you are going to be here that day, at three o'clock, and see how many of those fans come over to the park to hear you sing."

He got my message, I think. Looking back, I probably would have handled myself differently and not stood outside the press box. Over time, I let go of some things, but the wounds were still too fresh for me in the '80s.

At least the rest of the Cubs broadcasters were good guys. "Stoney" was coming along nicely in 1983. It's no secret that Steve went on to become one of the best analysts in our business and one of the best at his trade. After I left the Cubs in 1984, it hurt me for a long time that the two of us never spoke. It seemed he wouldn't speak to me because Steve feared that Harry might resent him for doing so. Steve could be a politician. During those early years, he wasn't going to do anything with me that Harry might hold against him.

Many years later, in Houston, I saw Steve in the Minute Maid Park press lounge and we enjoyed each other's company. "Stoney," I said, "wouldn't it be nice if we talked like this all the time? Wouldn't it be good if we went back to those earlier years?" And he said, "Milo, you're right." From then on, it was as if we were long-lost pals, like we were back working on the air again at Wrigley Field.

Steve's new attitude toward me might have rubbed off on Harry Caray's grandson, Chip Caray. Chip was in the Cubs booth following his grandfather's death, and during the 2003 season, he made many attempts to repair the damage between his family and mine. Chip would come over and slap me on the shoulder in the press lounge and ask about my wife's health. He knew Arlene was ill and always made it a point to ask about her. Chip's father, Skip Caray, has been horrible to me over the years just like Harry. It was refreshing to know that the grandson had decided to bury the hatchet. I can't tell you how much I appreciated that.

11

LEAVING ON A HIGH

On the playing field, my first four years back with the Cubs were more of the same losing ways that I had endured during my previous stint there when Ernie Banks was on the team. It was difficult at times to come to Wrigley Field and not be discouraged. But I looked to Jack Brickhouse for support, knowing that he was in the same boat during his 40-odd years in Chicago. He made it through a lot of losing campaigns, with the notable exceptions being the 1969 Cubs and the 1959 White Sox.

Jack still brought a refreshing approach with him to the park each game. He always did other things to entertain his listeners, which was his approach. Jack would parade luminaries through the booth game after game to keep the fans' interest day in and day out. I didn't go for that myself because I didn't have the same latitude as Jack with bringing dignitaries into the WGN booth.

Still, there were positive things to gravitate toward on the field of play. The focus of the 1982 season was watching Fergie Jenkins go for his 3,000th strikeout, which he achieved against San Diego in May. We knew Fergie was a future Hall of Famer, even if he was on the downside of his career at that time.

Ryne Sandberg got off to a horrible start at the plate in 1982, going 1-for-32. He was a third baseman then and we felt general manager Dallas Green would stick it out with him for the long haul. Dallas had known about Sandberg from the Philly organization and got him as the so-called "throw-in" in the deal that brought the Cubs shortstop Larry Bowa for Ivan DeJesus. Green was going to do everything he could to make sure this kid would succeed in Chicago.

As most fans remember, Ryne was quiet and very shy, which made him a tough man to interview. He wasn't the kind of player I wanted on my pregame show, but I respected his style and character. Ryne did things his own way, both on and off the field.

Contrary to some people's take on history, it was not Harry Caray who first dubbed Sandberg "Ryno." I was the creator of that nickname. I remember the first time I used it on air, we received some uncomplimentary mail from a few listeners, questioning if it was proper to use "Ryno," an animal name. But to me, it was a natural fit; Ryne Sandberg and "Ryno" went hand in hand.

By my fifth season with the team, things suddenly began to look bright. In many ways, my 1984 season with the Cubs resembled my broadcasting career as a whole—unlikely, unbelievable and unpredictable. The Cubs had finished in fifth place in the NL East in 1983. They ended up 19 games behind the division-winning Phillies with a 71-91 record—two games worse than in 1982. So expectations were not that high heading into 1984.

We were getting ready to leave Mesa, Arizona that spring when the Cubs traded for outfielders Gary Matthews and Bobby Dernier. That gave us the leadoff man we needed in Dernier and a clubhouse leader who had some power in Matthews. Two months into the season, we acquired Dennis Eckersley and, just three weeks later, Rick Sutcliffe. The dominos were falling into place: suddenly, a team that many figured to finish in the cellar was a pretty good-

Milo interviews the NL MVP of 1984, Ryne Sandberg.

looking outfit. We had Leon Durham, Ryne Sandberg, Ron Cey, Keith Moreland, Jody Davis, Matthews, and Dernier on the offensive side, and starters Scott Sanderson, Steve Trout, Sutcliffe, and Eckersley, with Lee Smith in the pen.

Sandberg got hot in June and never let up as he went on to win the NL MVP, batting .314 with 19 homers and an amazing 19 triples. He ignited the Cubs on June 23 in a Saturday matchup against St. Louis. With a national TV audience watching, Ryno went 5–for–6, drove in seven runs, and hit two dramatic homers off Cardinals closer Bruce Sutter to give the Cubs a 12-11 extra-inning win at Wrigley. His performance that day really sparked his MVP season and the Cubs as a whole.

Sandberg was inducted into the Hall of Fame in 2005, and if he hasn't already, he should send former Cards manager Whitey Herzog a bonus, because it was Herzog who proclaimed Ryno to be "Baby Ruth" after that June game. Herzog's comment got the nation's attention and helped to make Sandberg a household name.

But even more so than Sandberg's heroics, it was the Sutcliffe trade that convinced me the Cubs were for real and could beat out the Mets that summer. Getting him from Cleveland for Joe Carter and others was the turning point that year. When he came to us on June 13, he was 4-5 with a 5.15 ERA. But what a run that big horse had the rest of the year, going 16-1 with a 2.69 ERA to capture the Cy Young award. Imagine getting to a club in mid-June and going on to win the Cy Young!

The Cubs got on a roll in late August and just wouldn't fade in September, finishing 96-65 in manager Jim Frey's first season, including a 51-29 record at Wrigley Field. I really thought the Cubs were going to make it all the way to the World Series that year. Hindsight tells me that maybe the worst thing that happened in the National League Championship Series against the Padres was that the Cubs won the first game, 13-0. Sutcliffe pitched seven scoreless innings of two-hit ball, and also hit a home run at the plate. Steve Trout pitched well in Game 2 as the Cubs won again, 4-2. That meant we were headed to San Diego only needing to win one more game. A World Series meeting—the Cubs' first since 1945—with the Detroit Tigers was within reach.

Then the world caved in on us. The Padres turned into Cub Busters. I know a lot of people want to blame Leon "Bull" Durham for his error in Game 5, a miscue that paved the way for a four-run seventh inning after the Cubs had staked to Sutcliffe a 3-0 lead after six innings. Hey, Bull just flat-out missed that ground ball, like Bill Buckner did a few years later for the Red Sox against the Mets. It was one misplay, that's all, and it didn't cost the Cubs the chance of going to the World Series.

In my mind, I think the off day between Games 3 and 4 set the stage for our failure. We had won two big games at Wrigley Field and had the momentum working in our favor, but then we lost Game 3 in San Diego, 7-1, and had to sit around an extra day before playing again. Many of the players had brought their wives and families on that trip, and instead of hanging around the hotel and thinking about playing Game 4, some of the players felt obligated to go to Sea World, the San Diego Zoo, or somewhere else with the family. Somehow, we lost the flow or momentum, and became distracted.

It's sometimes the little things that can turn around a series in baseball. That is, if the big things—like Steve Garvey's game-winning homer in the bottom of the ninth off Lee Smith in Game 4—don't get you first. Ouch! That Garvey homer really swung the momentum back to San Diego. It tied the series up and gave the Padres the opportunity to win the series on their field in Game 5. The next day, San Diego stormed back from a 3-0 deficit to win, 6-3. Sutcliffe was roughed up in the seventh for four runs; meanwhile, the Padres bullpen threw seven and two-thirds innings of scoreless ball, allowing just two hits and one walk.

It was a tough flight back to Chicago after that October 7 game. Nobody talked on the plane and guys just sat in their seats, sleeping or staring ahead. By the time we arrived at O'Hare in the wee hours, Chicago was socked in with gloom—and some low fog. The mood of the city matched the atmosphere outside. The players quietly said their goodbyes for the season and were all off on their separate ways.

Little did I know that would be my last road trip with the Cubs. I didn't have an agent when I first came to the Cubs in 1982, but when WGN approached me at the end of that season about doing mostly radio, I got together with Brickhouse's old agent, Don Ephram. Don had approached me about the idea, and I figured that since he had worked with Brickhouse and WGN was familiar with him, he would be a good choice. As it turned out, Don got me a nice two-year deal that covered me through the end of the '84 season.

A few weeks after the season ended in San Diego, Ephram got a call from WGN to come down to the station. He figured they wanted to talk about a new contract, but instead he was blindsided. WGN told Don they were going to make a change to replace me, and that he had to get on the phone and deliver the bad news to me. WGN didn't make the call. Later I would learn it was once again the handiwork of Jim Dowdle, and that Caray had something to do with the decision as well. You can bet your mortgage "the Canary" orchestrated my firing.

Whether he would ever admit it or not, Caray resented the fact I had a decent following with Cub fans. He hated it when fans would approach me at the park to say hello or stop by to converse and say nice things. Some would come over and tell me how much they enjoyed my work, and how they would watch the game on TV, but turn the volume down on their television and listen to the radio broadcast. Caray would be within earshot, and "the Canary" only had to hear that once or twice before he was ticked. That used to really get to him. Finally, I suspect that he had enough and went to Dowdle and told him to get me out of town.

This marked the third time in my life that Caray had caused me to lose my job. He did so first in St. Louis in 1954, second when Dowdle brought him in to take over the lead job for the Cubs in 1982, and third at the end of the 1984 season. Dowdle must have felt a bit guilty again, because he surprisingly asked me to stay at WGN to handle the basketball broadcasts that winter for DePaul and the Bulls. Normally, when a radio or TV station asks an announcer to leave, they expect the announcer to come in that night and clean out his or her desk. They never want to hear the announcer on their airwaves again. That's how it is in our business. Well, not only did WGN want me to stay and do basketball games, but they also tore up my old basketball contract and tripled my salary! That's right, tripled it. Was that a pang of conscience on the part of Dowdle or what?

One day, not long after that, I dropped by WGN to get some things for my next basketball trip and ran into Wayne Vreisman, the station's general manager. Wayne was a decent guy, but kind of a milquetoast. He saw me inside and asked if I wanted to go to lunch. I said, "Why don't I drop by your office first?" because I wanted everyone inside the station to see me walk into his office. Right on his desk was a huge stack of fan mail, most of it addressed to me. Vreisman would not look directly at me, instead choosing to stare out the window as he spoke. I could tell he felt awkward about me seeing that stack of mail on his desk. "You know, Milo, you were really popular here," he said. "The salesmen here really liked you."

I just smiled. I had gone out of my way to help out the WGN salesmen over the years, showing up at requested functions to speak. Caray would never do those kinds of things. They were beneath him. If the Cubs needed someone to narrate their annual highlight film, I would be the guy the Cubs public relations director or marketing director would ask. Same thing when it came to the annual Welcome Home Luncheon or the Cubs Wives affair at Northwestern Memorial Hospital. Caray would never show for any of them.

The Cubs didn't like the idea that WGN was letting me go, and both president Jim Finks and general manager Dallas Green were in my corner. So was Bob Ibach, the public relations director who worked with me on a day-to-day basis; Jeff Odenwald, the marketing director; and Frank Maloney, the ticket manager. They all knew what I was going through with Caray. They knew the real story and the reason for my dismissal.

After the firing, Green called Dowdle and asked him to visit him at Wrigley Field. Then, one by one, he paraded Ibach, Odenwald, and Maloney into his office and, in front of Dowdle, asked each department director to describe what I had meant to the Chicago Cubs. I had to laugh because after he got all of their glowing reports, Dowdle turned to Green and said, "What are you doing, trying to railroad me?" And I'm told Dallas looked at him and said, "No shit."

Finks had another plan. The team had to give full approval to the hiring of any WGN broadcaster, and Finks was very upset about my dismissal. I was told his plan was to nix every Dowdle candidate, until Dowdle yelled uncle and took me back. I heard about that plan and in the back of my mind I still held out some hope that I might someday return to the Cubs booth. I was driving home a few nights after learning of Finks' plan, when I heard over the radio that Finks had just resigned as Cubs president after a meeting at the Tribune Tower. Talk about your heart sinking! There went my last hope of remaining with the Cubs. If I wanted to continue to do baseball, I would need to look elsewhere. So I began my job search.

It was getting close to the holiday season and that meant the annual WGN Christmas party was right around the corner. I had been invited to the lavish event despite losing the Cubs position, because I was still doing the basketball games. I went to the party, and Dowdle walked right up to me. I thought he would try to avoid me, but instead he came over to me and in his cheery voice said, "Milo, how are things going?" I couldn't believe it, and I wasn't about to mince any words. I looked right into his face and said, "How the hell do you think things are going? I'm outta work, pal, and it's a tough world out there." Then I walked away.

Shortly after the party, Odenwald, the Cubs marketing director, called me to ask a favor. He needed someone to narrate the Cubs' 1984 highlight film and asked if I would lend my voice to the video. Of course, if Odenwald was asking, I was willing to do it. I had known Jeff for many years, going back to when he was a kid at Ohio State and later working in the Atlanta Braves farm system. I treated him pretty well, and he never forgot it. Of course, when Caray heard of Odenwald's decision to have me on the film, he was pissed. But Odenwald wouldn't back down: I was his man.

While I was completing my work on the film, the Cubs announced they had hired Houston Astros broadcaster Dewayne Staats to take my spot. It was January at that time, and the Cubs were preparing for their annual caravan, where they would visit 10 neighboring communities in a week to spread the news about the upcoming season and to get folks excited about buying tickets. The Hot Stove week launched with the showing of the highlight film that I had narrated at the Stadium Club inside Wrigley Field. I was invited to attend the opening, as was Staats. It was the first time the media and the team's sponsors had seen the film.

The tape was well-received. There was a nice round of applause and some of the media and sponsors stopped by my table to tell me how much they had enjoyed my work. Staats came over and said to me, "Gosh, you were really popular here!" I had to chuckle to myself as I held a thought under my breath.

In closing this chapter of my life, I want to get something off my chest and set the record straight about an incident that followed Caray's death in February 1998. When he died, my response was to remain silent and say nothing. I didn't want any comments to be misconstrued, and I didn't want to be quoted for fear of someone twisting a quote around. But then I got a call from an Internet media person out of New York, asking for my reaction. I could sense that he wanted me to say something negative and told him I would not do that.

Years before, a magazine out of South Florida had called me soon after I took the Houston job in 1985. The magazine wanted to do a story on me and part of it was going to center on my relationship with Caray. I would never have agreed to do it had it not been for a TV interview that Caray had done that same winter on Channel 11, the public television station in Chicago, shortly after I was fired. All winter long, I had resisted the urge to talk openly about my firing. I never blamed Caray or said boo. But then Caray went on that TV show and for a full hour it turned into a Milo Hamilton roast. He really laid me out on the air.

If Caray had felt it necessary to disgrace me on the air— again—after I lost my job in Chicago, then all bets were off. Remembering the other times he had ripped me over the years, I felt it was time to have my say. So I opened up to this Florida magazine. I told the reporter how Caray had treated me in St. Louis in the '50s, and how he had ripped me on the air and in the papers when I was battling leukemia in the '80s. Caray felt I was a nobody and he could say what he wanted about me and get away with it. I was just fighting back.

The magazine article was published in 1985. Caray died 13 years later and the Internet reporter was grilling me over the phone, trying to get me to bite and talk negatively about Harry. The Internet was still in its infancy in 1998, and I'd never been an Internet person. So I figured that nobody was going to read my comments. I told the reporter that if he really wanted to know some of my feelings about Caray, he should look up that magazine article from 13 years ago—it was all there. Then I hung up.

That was a big mistake: the Internet reporter took the magazine article and that sonofabitch went ahead and wrote a story as if he were getting those quotes directly from me after Harry's death. The story received a lot of attention on the Internet, and Skip Caray got wind of it in Atlanta. He was so ticked off that he called the public relations director of Turner Broadcasting and got him to call a contact at The New York Times. Skip called me "insane" and "an idiot" and some other things. It was ugly.

When I arrived at the Astros spring training camp in 1998, the story had me in the middle of a big controversy, especially since the Braves trained close to the Astros in Central Florida. I tried to approach Skip to give him my side of the story, but he wasn't interested. He waved me away, which didn't surprise me. Skip is much like his father. He treats people around him like crap, a real chip off the old block. Just ask folks at Turner Broadcasting, WSB, or the ballpark in Atlanta: they'll tell you what he's like.

At least I know in my heart that I tried to set the record straight with Skip Caray. But he never listened.

12

TWO DECADES AND COUNTING IN THE LONE STAR STATE

C ubs general manager Dallas Green did not want to see me leave Chicago, but he also did not want to see me without a job. So he worked to help me land a new job in Houston. He called Astros general manager Al Rosen and said, "I know you're looking for somebody, and I've got just the person for you."

Rosen then called a meeting with the Astros director of broadcasting, the marketing director, me, and a few others. At the meeting—and in front of me—Rosen said, "I want an upgrade in our broadcasts. I know Milo's reputation. Dallas Green tells me he's the best at what he does. I've got to go to another meeting, and when I come back I want you to tell me you've hired him." I thought, "My God, did I write that myself?" He couldn't have said it any better if I told him, "Here's what I want you to say."

It took a few days to iron out the details. The Astros never guaranteed me that I was going to be their No. 1 announcer, but they made it clear that I was in their future plans when they gave me a two-year contract that paid me double the salary of the guy I was replacing. Sure enough, I was in their future plans: I have been in Houston more than 21 years and counting, my longest stint with one team.

One of the benefits of remaining with one club for so long is the chance I've had to develop friendships with so many amazing players. When I arrived in 1985, Nolan Ryan was entering his sixth season with the Astros. He helped me fit into the Houston community through his golf tournament, which was held out at Columbia Lakes, a suburb of Houston. The event raised money for the Ryan Foundation, which gave scholarships and money to Alvin Community College. The Ryan Foundation is so successful that he quit hosting the golf outing a few years ago because the foundation is self-sustaining at this point.

He invited me to emcee the event in 1985, which was a lot of fun. Out of that came invitations to emcee other charity events and auctions. Nolan and I were only together for four years before he moved on to the Rangers, but we discovered that we had a lot of common interests, like hunting.

Ryan won 106 games for the Astros, including 12 during the 1986 season. The 1986 Astros may not have had the best record of all the Houston teams that I've seen because two of Larry Dierker's late '90s teams bested the '86 Astros' mark of 96-66. But it was still the best team to date of my broadcasting tenure, because it was the most professional and simply knew how to play the game right. The team was full of veterans, guys like Phil Garner, Denny Walling, Craig Reynolds, Alan Ashby, Terry Puhl, Jose Cruz, Nolan Ryan, Bob Knepper, Mike Scott, Dave Smith, Larry Anderson, Aurelio Lopez, and Danny Darwin. And we had some relatively young guys who were key contributors, too. Billy Doran was a good second baseman, Glenn Davis was our slugging first baseman, Billy Hatcher played center, Kevin Bass was in left, Jim Deshaies was a big part of our rotation, and Charlie Kerfeld came out of nowhere to become a key part of our pen. It was a team that knew how to win and was coached by a talented rookie manager in Hal Lanier.

Bass hit 20 home runs, had a team-best 184 hits, swiped 22 bases, and hit .311 for that club. He was a switch-hitter who played all three outfield spots during his career. He came to play every day, and he fit in well on a ballclub that knew how to win. He was part of our young nucleus, as was Davis, who was 25 years old in 1986 and already quite the home run hitter. He popped 31 home runs and drove in 101 RBI that season. Some of his teammates resented Davis's attitude toward the philosophy of the team and felt he was a bit selfish. But he was a big part of that 1986 team.

Bill Doran was another of our valuable young veterans. He was one of those little guys—a real battler—who got his uniform dirty every game. He had a little pop in his bat as well, and he could steal some bases, too. He was a victim of playing in the Ryne Sandberg era. Doran was overshadowed by Sandberg, whose reputation made sure he kept winning the Gold Glove award year after year. There were a couple of years when Doran should have won it. On that '86 team, he was a very popular player and a close friend of Nolan Ryan.

Speaking of popular players, Cruz had been a great hitter for the Astros for many years coming into the 1986 season. He turned 39 in August of 1986, but even though he was old and his career was on the decline, he was still a valuable part of that team. Until Jeff Bagwell and Craig Biggio passed him, Jose had held a lot of Houston club hitting records, which led to having his number retired by the team.

Ashby was in his eighth season as an Astro in 1986. He was a real workhorse behind the plate: he caught all 16 innings of that famous 1986 playoff game between the Astros and the Mets. He was a switch-hitter who had some dramatic home runs as an Astro—among the best in team history. He was voted best catcher of the Astrodome era, and he probably could have played another year or two despite putting in 17 seasons in the big leagues. Maybe he thought it was time in 1989. After retiring, a television station hired him to be an anchor. He tried that for a couple of years, then he got back into baseball as a manager in one of those bandit leagues down in the Valley. Then he managed for the Astros farm system in Kissimmee, Florida before being hired as bullpen coach by the big-league club. When Larry Dierker was named the manager in 1997, Ashby took his spot in the booth. I had tried to get Ashby in the booth even before that. I just thought he had all the tools it took to be a great broadcaster, and he has not let me down. I've had some pretty good partners over the years, but for his play-by-play and analysis, he is without a doubt my best partner.

The team was held together by the 1986 NL Manager of the Year, Hal Lanier, who had been a coach under Whitey Herzog with the Cardinals. As far as his managing style, he reminded me a little bit of Eddie Stanky. He was one step ahead of the opposing manager all of the time. In 1987 and '88, he was a victim of the organization and then-GM Dick Wagner. In 1986, Wagner made a couple of deals for veterans that benefited the club down the stretch. If they completed similar trades in '87 and '88, then Houston would have won more games those years and Lanier wouldn't have lost his job. Instead, they went backwards a little bit, and Lanier committed the cardinal sin of criticizing the organization for not helping the club. He was let go and has never received another managerial job at the big-league level since. There is some talk that maybe he was blackballed because he criticized management. But he's done well for himself in the independent Northern League.

For that one year in 1986, Lanier did a fabulous job. I've done games for some teams that didn't make it to the World Series but should have, and chief among them is that 1986 team. The playoff series against the Mets was a killer. I will never forget the 16-inning Game 6, which has since been eclipsed in terms of length by the Astros' NLDS-clinching 18-inning win over the Braves in 2005. Knepper had a shutout going into the ninth, but ran out of gas as the Mets tied the game on a bases-loaded sac fly before Smith could get the final of the inning. The Astros scored three runs in the bottom of the first inning and then didn't score again until the bottom of the 14th inning. After the Mets took a one-run lead in the top of the inning, Billy Hatcher hit a home run to send the game to the 15th frame. When Hatcher hit the home run, I thought we were going to win. But two innings later, the Mets struck for three runs to regain the lead. In the bottom of the 16th, we strung together some singles to score two more runs, but Bass struck out with the tying run on second to end the game.

We lost, and unfortunately that was the deciding game in the series. If we would have held on to that game to force Game 7, we had Cy Young winner Mike Scott, who had pitched brilliantly in the series, ready to go. That year, he owned the Mets in the playoffs. He had allowed just eight hits and one earned run over the course of two complete games, the first of which was a 14-strikeout performance.

Art Howe was hired to replace Hal Lanier in 1989. He struggled in Houston to field a winning team and never finished better than third in the standings. But that wasn't entirely his fault. Howe was a victim of the organization and its decision to rebuild from the ground up, so his record wasn't very good. Then he was the victim of new ownership. When Drayton McLane took over the franchise, he envisioned somebody who was more outgoing and fiery as the team's skipper. And that wasn't Art's way, so he was replaced by Terry Collins, who appealed to McLane because he was enthusiastic and a little pepper-pot.

Collins had good credentials, having managed successfully in the Dodger chain. He got off to a good start in 1994, the strike year, finishing just a half-game behind the Reds. He had the club right in position to win the division. Jeff Bagwell was the MVP that year, hitting .368 with 39 homers and 116 RBI in the strike-shortened season. Craig Biggio was in his prime then, too, as he hit .318 and swiped 39 bases. Plus, we had a pretty good pitching staff. But due to the strike, Collins didn't get an opportunity to test his team down the stretch or in the playoffs. He finished second the next two seasons as well. Not a lot of guys who finish second three seasons in a row get fired, but McLane felt it was time for a change.

I've thoroughly enjoyed the time I've spent with Biggio, who joined the team in 1988, and Bagwell, who became an Astro three years later in 1991. We acquired Bagwell in one of those pennant-drive trades near the end of the 1990 season, when we sent Larry Andersen to the American League East-leading Boston Red Sox. Bagwell was then in Double-A and nobody—except for our scouts—had ever heard of him.

As my old pal Jack Brickhouse used to say, "Don't ever judge a trade until after it's two years old." That was a pretty good rule of thumb. I wasn't surprised by the initial reaction: how could they get rid of Andersen and bring in a guy who's playing in Double-A? But it soon became evident when Bagwell arrived at spring training camp in 1991 that he could hit. Yogi Berra, who was then one of our coaches, suggested to Art Howe that we try him at first base instead of third base. Ken Caminiti was at third then and would have probably blocked Bagwell from making the big league roster.

Near the end of spring training, Howe summoned Bagwell to his office. And Bagwell figured that was the day he was going to find out he was going down to Triple-A. Instead, Howe threw a first baseman's glove at him and said, "Try this." Bob Robertson, the old first baseman with the Pirates, was in the organization and practically lived with Bagwell night and day to show him the footwork. Jeff took to his new position like a duck to water. He was the unanimous Rookie of the Year and a unanimous MVP a few years later. He just kept getting better every year.

The Astros have always been great at encouraging players to change positions. Look no further than Craig Biggio: he went from catcher to second base to the outfield, and then back to second. Matt Galante deserves the credit for Biggio's switch from catcher to second, not only for suggesting it but spending hours hitting Biggio ground balls. He took him over on a side diamond and wore him out every day during spring training.

Craig became an All-Star second baseman and Gold Glove winner. Plus, he began stealing bases like crazy in the mid-'90s. If he would have remained a catcher, the natural wear and tear on his body would have prevented him from stealing 50 bases in a season, as he did in 1998. Craig also became a big doubles hitter and a very good leadoff man, setting the National League record for leadoff home runs.

Houston slugger Jeff Bagwell talks with Milo before a game in 1991.

We had some good outfielders in those days, too. Billy Hatcher joined the team in 1986, but really blossomed a year later in 1987 when he hit .296 and stole 53 bases. He was one of those guys who always had a smile on his face, was great with the press, and cared about the fans. He remained with us until August of 1989, when we shipped him to Pittsburgh for Glenn Wilson.

In 1991, we promoted a pair of young outfielders named Steve Finley and Luis Gonzalez. Finley was one of my favorites. He was a terrific centerfielder who later in his career developed a home run stroke. When he was with us, he used his speed to leg out triples and steal bases. What I really appreciated about Finley was that he played hurt. That made him not only a fan favorite, but a favorite with broadcasters, coaches, and teammates. The proof is in the pudding: he's still playing good baseball in the year 2005 and has enjoyed some very productive years both in the field and at the plate. He's had a terrific career.

Luis Gonzalez was drafted by the Astros in 1988. He enjoyed two stints with Houston, from a cup of coffee in 1990 through part of the 1995 season, and again in 1997. Gonzalez was a pretty good hitter with the Astros, but he wasn't a power threat. Matter of fact, he was platooned on occasion while with Houston. So I was surprised when he went on to become a power hitter with the Diamondbacks. One of the things that allowed him to become a different hitter: he—along with other hitters—hired a personal trainer to teach him new ways to work out. Instead of just taking the winter off and then showing up at spring training, he chose to work out all the time. He learned how to strengthen his body the correct way. But still, I never imagined that he would hit 57 home runs in a season. What isn't surprising is that Gonzo was and still is a fan favorite. He still has a lot of friends in Houston even though he hasn't played here for several years.

When Ken Caminiti came up in 1987, he skipped Triple-A entirely. I've seen many of the great third basemen: Brooks Robinson, Billy Cox, Graig Nettles, the Boyer brothers. I'd have to add Ken to that list. He simply gave up his body. Of course, we had no idea at the time that he was giving up his body to drugs, too. The first time he was with us—from 1987 to 1994—there was no suspicion that he was using drugs. The second time around—in 1999 and 2000 after he returned from four very productive years with the Padres—the stories of his usage were pretty well known. He was still that dedicated guy who played hard every day. But then injuries caught up with him and began to take their toll. The ballclub felt that something was bothering him—maybe alcohol. I never heard them say drugs, but maybe they were suspicious. When they really wanted him to seek some help, he turned on them and thought they weren't being fair. And that led to the end of his career with the Astros.

We had some good pitchers during the Art Howe-Terry Collins years, too. When Darryl Kile was with our club, he was a very popular player. He had the looks of a movie star, and he was a great pitcher to boot. His 19-7 campaign—when he posted a

2.57 ERA—anchored our 1997 rotation and was a big factor in the team finishing in first place. We always thought he was going to have arm trouble at some time due to the way he threw, but he never did. He featured that devastating curveball—definitely one of the best in the majors. When he pitched his no-hitter against the Mets, New York manager Dallas Green said he had never seen a player dominate with a curveball for nine full innings the way Kile did in that game. The only thing more devastating than Kile's curveball was his death in 2002. Even though he had moved on to the Rockies and then the Cardinals, he was still cherished by his former teammates here in Houston.

Pete Harnisch was a battler who enjoyed three solid seasons for us in the early '90s. Before spring training in 1991, the Orioles shipped Harnisch, Curt Schilling, and Steve Finley to Houston in exchange for Glenn Davis. Two years later, we traded for Mike Hampton in a deal that involved no big names. Hampton's six seasons with the Astros were terrific. He was a little stubborn early on, always trying to throw the ball by everybody. But once he learned to use that good changeup and that slider/cutter down and in to get people out, Hampton became a legitimate ace. He was also very good with the glove and the bat. In 1999, his final season with us, he went 22-4 and finished second in the Cy Young race to Randy Johnson. He was traded the next offseason to the Mets along with Derek Bell in a deal that landed us Octavio Dotel.

Jose Lima was yet another great pitcher whom we acquired in a huge deal with Detroit in 1996 that also netted us Brad Ausmus. For two seasons—1998 and 1999—it was "Lima Time" when Jose took the mound. He loved pitching at the Astrodome, and it showed: he went 37-18 during those two years. But things changed drastically in 2000. When we arrived in Houston after spring training, Lima walked into our beautiful new ballpark in downtown Houston and said, "I can no pitch here. I can no pitch with these kind of walls." I recommended that he speak with some of the pitchers who had toed the rubber at Fenway, the old Polo Grounds, or Ebbets Field. They learned how to adjust to the dimensions and walls of the ballpark. But Lima couldn't make the change, and it ate him up. He never recovered once he convinced himself that he couldn't pitch at Enron Field—and went on to prove it by going 7-16 with a 6.65 ERA in 2000. He was the player most affected by our move out of the Astrodome.

Shane Reynolds was one guy who was homegrown. The Astros drafted Reynolds in 1999, and three years later he made his big league debut. He could be counted on for quality innings every start, which is partly why he was named our Opening Day starter a number of times. His time with Houston came to an abrupt end during spring training of 2003 after 11 seasons with the team. He reported to spring training after a long layoff from surgery. He thought all he had to do was show the team that he could pitch, and his roster spot was safe; he didn't realize that he was in the camp to make the team. But the last day or so of camp, the Astros let him go. He forgave the club eventually, but it was tough for him. I think both the team and Reynolds thought he would be an Astro for life.

My current broadcast partner, Alan Ashby, thinks the 1998 Dierker-led team, which set a franchise record for wins with 102, is the best team in Astros history. It featured the original Killer Bs—Bagwell, Biggio, and Derek Bell—plus Moises Alou and a pitching staff anchored by Randy Johnson, Jose Lima, and Billy Wagner. But that team didn't play well in their postseason match-up against the Padres. The fact of the matter was, Dierker didn't manage very well. He didn't understand how to use his bench.

Moises Alou was a monster at the plate that year—posting career highs in hits, home runs, and RBI—just as he was in 2000 and 2001, when he was healthy. Alou was a terrific, gifted player, but he was also an enigma unto himself. I don't mean that he wasn't dedicated to being a good player, but there was always some question about whether he would play hurt. He would show up late to the trainer's room to work on his injury, and there was always a shadow of doubt over whether his injuries were legit. I don't think the whole story has been told yet.

Derek Bell was a unique guy, too. He was a fun-loving person, and his eating habits were unbelievable. It wasn't unusual for Bell to show up in the clubhouse with a bag of burgers that he would eat before the game. Then, after batting practice, he'd have the clubhouse guy go out and get him an order of Kentucky Fried Chicken. His poor diet probably hurt his career in the long run. But when he played, he was a good delivery man: he could drive in runs. His success on the field filled his wallet with money, and boy did he spend it. He never saw a new suit or a pair of shoes he didn't like. In New York's garment district, guys push carts down the side streets full of clothes. There were always two or three guys pushing those carts into the hotels where we stayed. Their final destination: Derek Bell's room. During the five years he was with us, I don't think I ever saw him wear the same suit or same pair of shoes twice.

Billy Wagner was still establishing himself as one of the most dominant closers in the majors in 1998, when he saved 30 games. He was one of those guys drafted from a small college whom nobody had ever heard of, yet the Astros were smart enough to take him with the 12th overall pick of the 1993 draft. He was a big part of the Astros' success for many years, but he talked himself out of town. He was very critical of team ownership after the 2003 season. When we lost the wild card on the final day of the season, he stood in front of his locker and said some negative things that he couldn't retract. That wasn't the only reason he was traded, however; his big salary played a part, too. But Billy could be his own worst enemy. He proved that again in 2005 with the Phillies when he popped off as they struggled.

On the mound, though, Wagner walked the talk. He got by 99 percent of the time with high heat, which got the crowd going crazy when he pitched. Sometimes he'd throw three pitches in a row 100 miles an hour and maybe sprinkle in one at 101. The criticism of him was that he needed another pitch. So he came up with a fairly decent slider. But it was still the high heat that got batters out.

So Larry Dierker had plenty of talent to manage during his tenure in Houston. Everybody was surprised when the team took

Milo interviews Larry Dierker during an Old Timers Day game in 1988.

him out of the broadcast booth and made him the manager in 1997. He'd never talked about managing and nobody had ever mentioned him as a possible manager. He had no experience, but Tal Smith, the team president, talked to the owner and said, "He's a great communicator."

The networks didn't agree. Even before he became manager, he kept thinking that ESPN or FOX was going to jerk him out of the booth and give him a job doing national broadcasts. He felt the same way when he got fired as manager. But the call never game.

I didn't think he would be a great manager. His teams did well in spite of him. He did let the guys play, as they say, but ultimately a manager's got to make a difference in some games—and Dierker rarely did. He didn't possess the sort of savvy or strategy that led to winning, especially in the postseason. That's when a manager's moves become magnified. His coaches openly questioned or raised eyebrows about some of the moves he made. He left his starting pitchers in longer than most managers because as a pitcher he was used to pitching deep into games. But the game has changed since he was a pitcher. With a bullpen full of seventh-, eighth-, and ninth-inning pitchers, why flirt with disaster?

This is not to say that Dierker wasn't a good manager—he simply wasn't a great one. There were a couple of reasons why he lost his job. For one thing, he lost the club's support. After criticizing his players in the media, his players turned on him. Dierker wasn't really a great communicator. For example, he thought that Bagwell and Biggio ought to rest once in a while, but he never told them that upfront. So they'd come in and see their names missing from the lineup card on the wall and become upset. Biggio really took it hard.

I happened to be in the clubhouse in Pittsburgh following a pregame interview with Dierker when Biggio came storming in and lit up the place. He had just found out that he wasn't playing that day, and he lost his cool. I love Biggio, as a player and a person, but that day, he said some things he normally wouldn't say. The entire team was there, and Dierker was sitting in his office. We all said, "Dierk's gotta come out here, take Bigg in the office, shut the door, and clear the air." But Dierker never said boo. It was clear right then that he had really lost control of his team.

In 1998, Gerry Hunsicker was named Executive of the Year and Dierker was named Manager of the Year. The players thought Dierker received way too much credit. Later, as Dierker's worth started to diminish in his players' eyes, some of them said, "The worst thing that ever happened to Dierker was when he won the Manager of the Year award." Those were pretty damaging reflections by guys he was counting on to go to battle for him.

He lost the coaches, too. He had so much pride that he wouldn't wear hearing aids even though he was going deaf. So when the bench coach or pitching coach would tell him, "Dierk, we gotta make a move here," he often didn't hear them. By the time he finally understood, it was too late. They finally just asked themselves, "What are we doing?"

His nickname was Sluggo, because he was always spilling coffee all over his scorecard or tripping down the steps coming into the booth. He was just clumsy. One day, he injured himself near the Drake Hotel in Chicago when he crashed while skating on rollerblades back to the hotel from Wrigley Field. But it was no joke when he had a seizure in the dugout during a game in June of 1999. People thought he'd had a heart attack and was dying in the dugout. Craig Biggio, a very religious man, called for Gene Pemberton, the club chaplain, to lead them in prayer on the field. Matt Galante ran the club for about a month, but Dierker recovered and returned to the dugout.

After he was fired, Dierker wrote a book titled This Ain't Brain Surgery, which was a reference to the near-fatal seizure he had. He told a lot of great stories and it was an interesting book. As the publication date neared, I saw him and said, "How's the book coming?" He replied, "It's coming along. It's coming out soon."

I heard more about it at the 2003 R.E. Bob Smith Rotary Baseball Player of the Year dinner. Solly Hemus, one of Dierker's friends, brought Dierker along as his guest at the dinner. I asked Larry about the book before the dinner. He said, "It's coming out next week." And I said to myself, "Good. Tonight when I introduce him, I'll introduce Larry Dierker, former great pitcher, manager, and broadcaster, who's got a book coming out next week."

He knew I was going to introduce him, and it would have been a perfect opportunity for him to say to me, "There's some things I wrote in there about you that you may not like." But he gave me no warning. Again, he's hardly a great communicator.

So the book came out, and I learned that he made fun of me about a lot of different things. He said that I wore my Hall of Fame pin too much. He said that I gave out too many Hall of Fame baseball cards. And he wrote some other things that just weren't complimentary. I'm not as upset about what he wrote as I am that I didn't find out about it from him—before the book was released. My son bought the book because he heard about it. He called me one day and said, "Dad, have you seen the Dierker book?" I said, "No." He said, "You aren't going to like it." He read me some of the stories and I couldn't believe it. After all that I had done for Dierker as a broadcaster and later a manager, and this is how he chose to thank me? It just didn't make sense.

In 1992, a few months before I went into the Hall of Fame, he had written a column about "captains of the airwaves" for the Houston Chronicle. He said that by his definition, "captains of the airwaves" are the sort of broadcasters who carry fans to games. He talked about legends like Jack Buck and Vin Scully, and he discussed how I prepared for games, how I poured my heart and soul into the games, and how the clarion Hamilton voice always rang true. "Hamilton is a beauty," he wrote. "He fills more dead air than maybe all the other great broadcasters. He brings in more counterpoints and gets the crowd into it more. And he does it all within the formal description of good reporting."

Dierker had given me the nickname Captain. Now a lot of people call me Captain, mostly fellow broadcasters and people at the ballpark. When we used to change booths during a broadcast, I would go back on the air and Dierker would say, "Now here's the captain of our crew, Milo Hamilton." And the name stuck. So in the final paragraph of his column, he wrote, "Buck and Scully have been voted into the broadcaster's wing of the Baseball Hall of Fame and Captain Hamilton is waiting for the call, which should be coming soon."

That was just a few months before I was voted in. It was in August of '91 and I got voted in seven months later, in March of 1992. When I was elected Houston Sportsman of the Year, Dierker was the emcee and talked about me in glowing terms. He said how much I had helped him as a broadcaster, and told me how all of his friends, like Hemus and Bob Aspromonte, felt I nurtured him as an analyst.

When Dierker's book came out, Kenny Hand, a former writer, asked him, "Dierk, why did you write that stuff about Milo?" And his answer was, "Because my publisher told me I needed somebody to help me sell the book, to make it controversial." I tried to get him to meet me to give him a chance to tell me why he wrote those things. But all Dierker did was duck me. When the meetings were arranged, he wouldn't show up.

The book came out in July of 2003. Finally, a couple of months into the 2004 season, he showed up for a meeting. He came in, sat down, and said, "I guess we really should have had this meeting a long time ago." And I said, "No shit."

He said, "I've heard that your son is really upset with me." And I said, "You've understated that phrase."

I added another thought: "You know," I told him, "you've stiffed me for months now. We could have gotten this out of the way a long time ago or right after the book came out."

I asked him, "Why me? Why did I have to be the guy you picked on?" His reply: "Because my publisher said you're the biggest name in town. I had to do it with somebody big so it would draw attention to help sell the book."

Then he said, "I think maybe your son overreacted." I replied, "Well, you ain't my son. Imagine how your son would feel if I wrote those things about you in my book after telling everybody how great I thought you were."

At the end of the conversation, I told him that we should just put this all behind us—that it was over as far as I was concerned. It's not like I could collect all of his books and burn them. People had bought the book, and that was that. For me, the case was closed. I was disappointed. He owed me more than that for the way I respected him as a broadcaster and a baseball star. To make me the brunt of jokes in his book and use the excuse that he did it to help sell books was not a fair deal. I told him it would be nice if he could apologize in one of his weekly columns. But I'm still waiting for that column.

A s for the 2004 team, we had high expectations because Roger Clemens had come home to Houston. Andy Pettitte, his former

Yankee teammate, was also signed as a free agent. Morgan Ensberg was coming off a breakout season, and Adam Everett was blossoming as a shortstop. That team featured a revised Killer Bs attack in Bagwell, Biggio, and Lance Berkman. When they added a fourth B—Carlos Beltran—near the trading deadline, the lineup looked imposing. Our pitching staff was handled expertly by Brad Ausmus, and in addition to Clemens and Pettitte featured 20-game winner Roy Oswalt and one of the NL's best closers in Brad Lidge. Lidge is a hard thrower just like his predecessor, Billy Wagner. Lidge throws 97-98 mph and once in a while will hit 99. Just as the batter gets dialed up for that heat, Lidge will throw one of the nastiest sliders in the game. In terms of the number of great pitches and how he uses them, Lidge has surpassed Wagner because he keeps the batter guessing—there's no sitting on a particular pitch.

Jeff Kent contributed his usual 100 RBI and broke a few records in 2004. But that didn't make him any easier to deal with. Jeff was in a world of his own, a real Jekyll-and-Hyde personality. When we went on the Astros caravan and made stops at hospitals, he would knock their socks off. He was spectacular with kids— they thought Jeff Kent hung the moon. If we went to a high school, he talked to the football team or the baseball team and was incredibly charming. But Jeff didn't like the media and was very upfront about that. When he got to the ballpark and put on that uniform, he was a different guy. He would not appear on our pregame show, and I always felt that it just wasn't right. A ballplayer owes it to some people to occasionally do things for them.

When Kent passed Rogers Hornsby for home runs by a second baseman, I went up to his locker after the game to shake hands and he asked me, "Who's Rogers Hornsby?" I said, "Only the greatest righthanded hitter of all time, and you just broke his second-base home run record." He said, "I don't care about that. When I quit, I'm not going to have anything to do with baseball. Those things don't mean anything to me."

In 2004, we were in Milwaukee when he set a new Astros record by hitting in 25 consecutive games, breaking Tony Eusebio's team mark. Again, I went to his locker after the game congratulated him, and once again he said, "That don't mean nothing to me." He wouldn't shake hands. Then he broke Ryne Sandberg's record for career home runs by a second baseman—which, a year or two ago, I thought might stand forever. I said, "Will you shake hands now?" He said, "What did I do now?" I said, "You didn't hear the crowd when you hit that home run and they put it up on the big goddamn message board that looks like a train car?" He said, "Yeah, I guess."

Kent was always the last guy on the bus when we were going to the ballpark. He timed it perfectly. I sat toward the front of the bus with the rest of the broadcasters. When Jeff got on the bus I always made it a point to loudly say, "Hey, Jeff, how're you doing today?" He would give me an "Mmmm" or nod begrudgingly.

So finally when he hit the big home run—a three-run walkoff home run in Game 5 of the 2004 NLCS—I walked up to his locker and said, "Now I won't accept no. You've got to let me shake your hand." He did and he smiled. Why was that so tough? I just don't understand Jeff Kent.

It took not one, but two managers to keep the 2004 team headed in the right direction. Jimy Williams, who started the 2004 season as manager before being replaced by Phil Garner at the All-Star break, was a great skipper. In 2003, he had kept an injury-stricken team in the race until the last week of the season. He was the best manager in terms of instructing that I have ever been associated with. His spring trainings were a sight to see. On some teams, the manager simply stands on one diamond with a fungo bat in his hands. But Williams was everywhere—always teaching, teaching, teaching. He was constantly trying to make people better.

Jimy would never say anything bad about his players. In fact, he really stood up for them, which was a direct contrast to Dierker, who lost his team by being critical of them in the media. But there was just a little something missing in Jimy's makeup. And that little something was what Phil Garner brought to the club. Maybe it was simply enthusiasm. For Garner to manage a club he played for, in a town that is his adopted home, meant a lot to him.

But success didn't happen overnight for Garner once he joined the club. During his first two weeks we dropped further under .500. But then things started to click and the team began winning

Houston manager Phil Garner shares a laugh with Milo prior to a 2005 game.
Stephen P. O'Brien

games. He energized the team's running attack, focusing on stolen bases and putting runners in motion. Utilizing bunts, suicide squeezes, and double steals (of which we had seven after the All-Star break), Garner placed an emphasis on being aggressive on the bases.

The team reflected the way Garner played. I gave him his nickname "Scrap Iron" when he was with the Pirates because his uniform was always dirty. He dove for balls. He couldn't run a lick and he stole more than 30 bases three times. He was a manager's best friend: he had a great outlook, he was always thinking, and he was very sharp, and if there was a fight, he was the first one there.

The "Scrap Iron" theme worked well for the team in 2004. The team bought into the style of play and played their fannies off for Garner. Then they brought up Brandon Backe. What a lift he gave our rotation, especially in the postseason. As the pitching staff settled down, the offense took off as Beltran became a valuable cog in the machine, running the bases and hitting for power. He gave us the centerfielder the club hadn't had since Steve Finley. Everything just clicked.

We roared down the stretch with a 36-10 record, passing five teams to grab the wild card. We lost just seven times in September, and won our last seven games of the season. As the season wound down, we took it to the Cardinals, winning five of our last six games against them. And we beat the Brewers, Reds, and Cubs like a drum. The secret was not to lose a series. It was all right to lose a game, but the trick to gaining ground was to not drop an entire series.

The amazing thing about that run was that the Astros were really doing all that winning with only two starting pitchers: Clemens and Oswalt. They were spot-starting Pete Munro, Tim Redding, and later Backe, who came to Houston before the season in a deal that sent Geoff Blum to Tampa Bay. Backe was a shortstop and an outfielder in the Tampa Bay system but wasn't hitting a lick. It became evident that he was never going to get to the big leagues as a position player, but since he had a great arm, somebody had the foresight to convert him to a pitcher. Backe pitched some big games for us down the stretch, and the town just fell in love with him. If somebody had said in the middle of August that Brandon Backe was going to be a factor in winning the wild card, I'd have said, "You're nuts." Yet he showed more guts than a Missouri mule.

Once we made it into the postseason, we beat the Braves in the Division Series, then took the Cardinals to the seventh game of the

Championship Series. I really thought that when Kent hit the walk-off home run to win Game 5, the Cardinals wouldn't recover. But they did. Still, making it into the Championship Series gave the team a big lift; the Astros were used to losing in the first round, especially against Atlanta. Of course, that trend has changed over the past two years, as Houston has knocked Atlanta out of the playoffs two years in a row.

I've changed my mind about the wild card. When it was first introduced, I was one of those purists who thought that teams that don't finish first in their division shouldn't play in the postseason. But it has created excitement in so many cities by keeping teams alive.

A fter the 2004 Astros won the wild card with a 36-10 stretch drive, I thought I had seen one of the great single-season comebacks in baseball history. Never did I think they could do it again, especially after Carlos Beltran and Jeff Kent left as free agents. That was a lot of offense to replace, especially with Lance Berkman on the mend to start the 2005 season.

My worst fears were confirmed when the team got off to a dreadful start in 2005. I wondered whether we could catch lightning in a bottle again. I wouldn't have any credibility remaining if I told you that I thought the 2005 Astros were destined for the World Series when they were 15-30 on May 24. The ray of hope that I held onto at that time was that our pitching was good enough that we could have been 30-15. But we weren't hitting a lick. We were last or next to last in the league in most of the important offensive categories. But we knew that if this team would ever start hitting, it could be dangerous.

Three people were guiding lights for us at that low point in the season: our owner, Drayton McLane, our general manager, Tim Purpura, and manager Phil Garner. A 15-30 start causes some owners to panic and run to the general manager screaming, "You've got to do something. Make a trade! Get rid of some of these minor-leaguers and get a hitter." But McLane didn't do that.

He had faith in his rookie GM, who had come through as an assistant to Gerry Hunsicker in player development. Purpura believed in the kids in the Astros system, guys like Willy Taveras, who skipped Triple-A on his way to sticking with the Astros in 2005. Taveras was our first prototypical centerfielder since Steve Finley, and Garner sent him out there every day. Taveras responded by hitting .291 and stealing 34 bases. For his efforts, he was named Rookie of the Year by The Sporting News.

Purpura also recognized the talents of Chris Burke. They gave him a second chance in 2005, and he responded with some memorable hits. The bullpen was another point of contention in the media, but Purpura stuck with them and they turned out to be a very effective pen. Management did not give up on this club, and in turn the club didn't give up either.

A lot of credit should also go to Garner, whose attitude kept the team afloat. I call him "Chuck Tanner Jr." because, like Tanner, Garner won't let a club quit. When the team was in the dumps, Garner told the players, "We're going to play one game at a time." That was his theme. First the team had to get back to .500, then it had to get over the hump for good. At that point, winning all of their series became the team's goal. When his players bought his message—that all was not lost—the positive thinking really permeated the team and provided them with a boost. Of course, the leadership on this team—guys like Biggio and Berkman—was incredible. Bagwell's attitude was phenomenal, too. After his surgery rendered him unable to help the club on the field, he told Purpura, "I want to be in uniform on that bench." He never swung a bat until after Labor Day, but he sure as heck contributed to the team's wild-card berth.

All the positive thinking in the world wasn't going to get us into the playoffs unless our offense came around. As we climbed back to .500 and then raced down the stretch toward the playoffs, our pitching remained solid and our offense finally showed signs of life. Berkman played a key role in that resurgence. He's followed the leadership of Biggio and Bagwell all these years, but in 2005 he really became a leader unto himself. Returning from his injury in May, Berkman needed time to find his groove. But when he did, he made a lethal 1-2 punch with Morgan Ensberg. When those two guys were on, they were one of the league's best power-hitting tandems. Together, they revitalized the offense and carried a lot of the load—along with Jason Lane and Mike Lamb.

Hitting is contagious, or at least it was for the Astros in 2005. As Lamb's playing time increased down the stretch in September, so too did his production. Lane also enjoyed the best second half of his young career in 2005 as he finished with 26 homers. Biggio bested his career mark set in 2004 by hitting 26 homers in 2005. It seems like Biggio passes up another big name in the record books on a monthly basis.

Someone we don't talk about enough is Brad Ausmus. Simple statistics do not represent what he means to this team. He saves the manager a trip to the mound because he serves as a manager from behind the plate. I've heard that from three of his managers, and I've heard that from a future Hall of Famer in Roger Clemens, who gives him all the credit in the world. In fact, the night we presented Clemens with his seventh Cy Young Award at home plate, he pointed right to Ausmus in the dugout and said, "I couldn't have won this Cy Young Award for 2004 if I didn't have Brad Ausmus as my catcher." That speaks volumes.

Ausmus is an incredibly smart catcher, and he knows how to call a game. He gets the most out of the pitcher. If the pitcher falls in love with a certain pitch or if he's rushing his pitches, Ausmus heads to the mound to discuss the situation. His preparation before the game is phenomenal, too. He's a computer whiz, and he uses technology to prepare and study scouting reports. Garner gives him a lot of credit for preparing a pitching staff for a series.

Preparation is important, but so is performance. And in 2005, the core of our pitching staff was spectacular—and full of surprises. First, there was the surprise of Andy Pettitte returning from elbow surgery and being so sharp. Pettitte, who is not a braggadocious person, admitted that he had a stellar second half as he went 11-2 with a 1.69 ERA after the All-Star break.

Then there was the surprise of Clemens not only returning for another year, but also leading the world with a 1.89 ERA. Clemens finished the season pitching through a chronic hamstring and groin injury, making his performance all the more special. The injury had been bothering him for the final six weeks of the season, and then on into the playoffs. He told me, "I'm finding out I don't heal as fast as I used to." Most 43-year-olds don't. But due to his work ethic, his dedication, and his grind-it-out attitude, he had one of the best seasons of his career. That attitude is something that the younger pitchers can learn from. Having Clemens on this team will benefit the Astros for years to come.

A third surprise occurred on the final day of the season, when Roy Oswalt posted his second straight 20-win season. Oswalt recorded some tough losses due to a lack of run support. But like the rest of our starters, he didn't say boo about it. He never put it on the team for failing to score.

The season-long turnaround might have been for nothing if the Astros wouldn't have won their final game of the year. In doing so, they made certain to avoid a play-off game against Philadelphia for the wild-card berth. Oswalt outdueled Greg Maddux and the Cubs, and Lidge saved the 6-4 victory, to ensure the Astros of our second-straight wild-card berth. Waiting for us in the first round of the playoffs was our old nemesis, the Braves.

Once again, everyone figured us to be the underdog in the NLDS. But our offense came up big for us as we scored a total of 24 runs in our three wins. And in Game 4, we collected our biggest hits of the season. Down 6-1 in the eighth inning, the Astros loaded the bases for Berkman, who brought them all home with an opposite-field grand slam into the Crawford Boxes. Then in the bottom of the ninth, Ausmus homered off Kyle Farnsworth to tie the game up and send it to extra innings. It was probably the longest home run he'd ever hit. From there, the bullpen held the Braves scoreless until Burke could step up to the plate in the bottom of the 18th inning.

Clemens, who had taken the loss in Game 2, was called on in the 16th inning. He had realized that the game was going to drag on and that he might have to pitch in relief. Clemens called on his son Koby, who signed with the Astros that summer, to come down out of the stands to lend a hand. Clemens told his son, "We've got to go down to the tunnel and I've got to pitch to you." The kid said, "Why don't I grab a bat and you'll throw to me like I'm hitting? We'll play our old game of One Ball, One Strike." Clemens ended up throwing 40 pitches before sneaking out to the bullpen. When he arrived, Stretch Suba, the bullpen coach, said, "You're up next. Do you want to throw some?" Clemens said, "I don't think I'll need to." He got into the game as a pinch-hitter, then pitched three scoreless innings. Clemens was pitching on pure guts. He thought, "I'll just let it fly." And boy, did he ever.

That set the stage for Burke's walk-off home run. That home run was one of the most dramatic home runs that I've ever seen. And it barely made it out. Burke sailed around the bases and leapt onto home plate. I've called a lot of extra-inning games that ended dramatically, but this one was special since we were in the spotlight of a playoff game. Considering the opponent, the home run was even more significant. The Braves were supposed to eliminate us, but instead we eliminated them with one swing of the bat. Baseball sure is the most unpredictable game in the world.

The 2005 NLCS was sweet redemption after losing to the Cardinals in the 2004 NLCS. But it wasn't without its gut-wrenching moments. We were a pitch away from ending Game 5, with Lidge on the mound. Then the pesky David Eckstein hit a seeing-eye single through the infield. That brought Edmonds to the plate, and that's where Lidge made his biggest mistake—not going right after Edmonds. Instead, Lidge walked him. Alan Ashby and I had mentioned a couple of innings earlier how important it was to make certain that Albert Pujols would not bat again in the ninth. But that walk to Edmonds enabled Pujols to come to the plate as the go-ahead run.

In any given month, Lidge probably doesn't throw two hanging sliders. But unfortunately, in the bottom of the ninth inning of Game 5, with a trip to the World Series on the line, he threw two in that inning: one to Eckstein that was hit through the infield, and one to Pujols that was hit to the Gulf of Mexico. You talk about getting it all—Pujols crushed that hanging slider and sent the series back to St. Louis.

But the Astros remained focused. Their calling card all season long was resiliency. As tough as that loss was—and it was a ballbuster—it didn't destroy their spirits. Besides, they had Oswalt taking the mound in Game 6, and he already had determined that St. Louis was not going to beat him in that game. He absolutely shut down the Cardinals, sending Houston to its first-ever World Series to face the Chicago White Sox.

The White Sox almost blew a 15-game divisional lead in the month of September. But after sweeping their divisional foe, the Indians, to finish the season, they were warming up at just the right time. They had swept the defending champion Red Sox in the ALDS, and after losing the opener to the Angels in the ALCS, they took four in a row from them. They were on a roll.

Still, I thought we really had a shot at them. But that series, and especially the final game, really mirrored our team in 2005: great pitching, no clutch hitting. Without our offense coming up big for us, we were doomed. Chicago had great pitching just as we did, but they also produced some really timely hitting and advanced runners when necessary. In the series sweep, Berkman drove in six runners, but the rest of the Houston offense couldn't come up with enough big hits. I have to tip my hat to the White Sox, who out-hit and outpitched us. But I'm still proud of this 2005 Astros team. They had a hell of a season.

"HOLY TOLEDO" AND OTHER MILOISMS

"Holy Toledo" is my signature call, but it came about quite by accident. Its origins date back to my first week of announcing baseball, in 1950 in the old Three-I League in Davenport. There was a great play on the field and I said, "Holy mackerel, what a play!" I absolutely swear I had never said "holy mackerel" before in my life.

Some listeners weren't too excited about my ad-lib. The town I grew up in—Fairfield, Iowa—had a little Catholic church, with maybe 50 or 100 people in the parish. "Holy mackerel" wasn't an insulting remark, but it was something that people talked about in the 1930s. Catholics had to eat fish on Fridays. As a result, when certain ignorant people referred to Catholics, they called them "mackerel snappers." It was a derogatory term. In Davenport and in the Quad Cities, there was a Catholic church on every corner—

not just a small parish like in my little town of 7,000. Those people took exception to "holy mackerel."

I'd never before received a negative letter from a listener. And there were several. Maybe they ganged up on me. I said, "Boy, if they feel that strongly about it, I don't think I ought to ever say that again."

I used to love to sit around and listen to my dad and his pals talk around the big coal stove as they'd smoke and tell stories. My dad and his friends weren't religious people, but they did have a code that they never swore. I never heard my dad say a bad word. The little game they played was if there was ever an instance where they might blurt something out, they would say "Holy Toledo" instead.

The phrase wasn't singular to them because it was a Midwest thing. I heard it from a lot of people. So I thought maybe "Holy Toledo" would work instead of "Holy mackerel." I began to incorporate it into my broadcasts, and no one ever complained. That was in 1950, and I've been using it ever since. Of course, I reserve the phrase for the truly magnificent play, so that the fans know that it was a remarkable feat.

An announcer can't remember everything that happens in a game, so in order to provide an accurate recap, I make special notations on my scorecard. If a great play is made, I put a blue star by it. If the shortstop made a great play in the field, next to the "6" on the card I place the star. The next time the shortstop comes up to bat, I might say, "Boy, in the third inning Adam Everett made a fantastic play in the hole to get Reggie Sanders at first. It was a blue-star play!" Rather than just use the star on my scorecard, I began to work it into my delivery. Now, when one of those plays happens, people down in the stands will turn up to the booth and ask, "Milo, did you put a blue star on that baby?" It has become something that they anticipate.

It has become such a big deal that we even got a sponsor out of it. Chris Luke of Metal Sewing Technology Company and Yvette Csares, who sells advertising for the Astros, got together and said, in a kidding kind of way, "Why don't you sell that blue-star thing?" Sure enough, it seemed like a good idea. So now, maybe once or twice a game we'll say, "And there's a Metal Sewing Technology

blue-star play." It turned out to be a pretty good deal for both the team and the sponsor.

Ray Buck wrote one of my favorite articles in the Houston Post when I went into the Hall of Fame. He included a sidebar in which he cited 10 of my favorite sayings, listed here in no particular order.

HOTTER THAN A DEPOT STOVE. Anybody who grew up in the Depression in the 1930s or maybe even the '40s probably had a train that went through town. There was a depot that always had a potbellied stove in the foyer. It burned so brightly at night that it heated the potbelly, and as you went by it glowed in the dark. The saying in my hometown about that was "hotter than a depot stove." So when a guy's on a real hitting tear or playing in a double-header and he's gone 6-for-8, I say, "Boy, he's hotter than a depot stove."

LOOSER THAN SHELL CORN. Growing up in a Midwest farming community, big bushel baskets of shell corn were a common sight. If you dug your hand into the basket and tried to grab the corn, it would trickle through your fingers. When I talk about a player who seems to be under no pressure in a game and really looks like he's relaxed, I say, "Boy, that guy is looser than shell corn."

FLIP FOR ONE, FIRE FOR TWO. As a double-play is being turned, I'll often say, "Ball's hit to short—flip for one, fire for two." And then come back out of that and say, "That's a six, four, three." But the phrase that lets you know it's going for the double-play is, "Flip for one and fire for two."

JUG-HANDLE LINE DRIVE. This particular saying makes reference to the curved handle of a jug. Line drives that go straight are often just off the ground. Some people call them "humpback liners." But a jug-handle line drive is one that's got a big loop in it. It's hit hard enough to be a line drive but has a curve to it. "Biggio smacks a jug-handle line drive to left, right over the shortstop's head."

SCREAMIN' MEEMIE. This is my saying for a line drive that must have hair on it—it buzzes through the infield right past an infielder. The ball will go by the shortstop or the second baseman or right by the pitcher's ear.

BASEBALL, THE MOST UNPREDICTABLE GAME IN THE WORLD. I got this one from my mentor and idol Bob Elson. He used to say, "This game—you see it and you think you've seen it all. You can do it for years and you can see games, and there's always something you'll see that's different. Baseball is truly the most unpredictable game in the world."

THE BALLPARK WILL NEVER HOLD IT. If there's a long drive and it's obvious from the minute it leaves the bat that it's going to be a home run, my expression is "The ballpark will never hold it." Before it gets out, the fan knows it must have really been hit hard.

LEAPIN' LENA. A leapin' Lena is a high hopper that goes over the pitcher's mound and over second base. It's as if the ball is leaping. So if you hear "leapin' Lena," you know the ball jumped over the pitcher's mound and headed out to center field, and neither the shortstop nor the second baseman could field it.

EYELASH CALL AT FIRST. An eyelash is a very thin hair, so when a guy is out at first on a bang-bang play, I say it was an "eyelash call at first."

STEPS ON THE PAY STATION is just another way of saying steps on home plate. For a runner, it pays off when he hits home plate. I might say, "He just crossed the pay station with the second run of the night."

HOLY TOLEDO. And of course, my signature call for a great play.

CALLS TO REMEMBER: NO-HITTERS, RECORD BREAKERS, AND DIVISION CLINCHERS

I've been behind a big-league microphone for more than a half-century, so I've seen more than my share of historic games and memorable plays. I certainly can't forget doing the first-ever Atlanta Braves game when they opened the 1966 season against the Pirates. That was a historical moment. Tony Cloninger was pitching, we had a sell-out crowd, and there were several dramatic home runs, including two by Joe Torre. Cloninger pitched a complete game, going 13 innings before the Pirates won 3-2 on a two-run Willie Stargell home run. The Atlanta fans had waited years for a major league team, so to be the announcer on that first game is definitely one of the highlights of my career.

Another memorable game was Mike Scott's no-hitter in September of 1986, in part because it clinched first place for the Astros. That was the first time that anyone had pitched a no-hitter in a division-clinching game since Allie Reynolds did it as a Yankee

Houston teammates Jim Deshaies, left, and Kevin Bass hoist Mike Scott into the air after his no-hitter clinched the divisional title for the Astros in 1986. *AP/WWP*

in the early '50s. Scott blanked the Giants, a fairly good-hitting club that featured Will Clark, Candy Maldonado, Chili Davis, and Robby Thompson. Clark made the last out for the Giants, and Scott finished the game with 13 strikeouts and two walks as the Astros won 2-0.

It was a remarkable performance by Scott, who just 18 months prior to that start had been told that his career was in jeopardy and that he might not even make the club because he didn't have an out pitch. That winter, Scott went to Roger Craig and learned the splitter. That pitch rejuvenated his career, and in 1986 he won the division-clinching game, threw a no-hitter, and won the Cy Young Award.

On the other end of the no-hitter spectrum was the Astros' collective no-hitter against the Yankees in June of 2003. It was the first no-hitter thrown against the Yankees since Hoyt Wilhelm, a spot-starter for the Baltimore Orioles, threw one in 1958. In a unique game, six Astro pitchers shut down the Yankees at Yankee Stadium. Our ace, Roy Oswalt, had a groin injury that had been ongoing and had to leave the game after making his warm-up tosses prior to the start of the second inning. So we had to go to our bullpen quite early in the game. Five relievers combined with Oswalt to complete the no-hitter. What were the odds of that? And what were the odds that one of those five, Octavio Dotel, would pitch one inning and have four strikeouts?

Brad Lidge pitched the sixth and seventh innings for the win, before Billy Wagner struck out two of the last three batters to finish the game. Houston pitchers combined for 13 strikeouts in the game, with only Pete Munro's three walks preventing them from pitching a perfect game.

It didn't dawn on manager Jimy Williams that he was watching a no-hitter until the game's later stages. "I'm looking up and I see this ballgame going along and we've got all those hits and runs," Williams told me. "Because I was using all those pitchers, I figured somebody must have had a hit for the Yankees."

I didn't mention the no-hitter on the air either. They don't use the word "no-hitter" in the dugout. It's a superstition that's good enough for the players, so it's good enough for me, too. If I had been a young announcer just starting out, I might have mentioned it on air. But there are so many ways to tell the fan that there's a no-hitter going on without using those words. For example, I can say, "There are only three hits in this game, and the Astros have them all."

In addition to those two no-hitters, I've seen nine others—but no perfect games. Something always seems to happen: a walk or an error, or the pitcher is just unlucky. Like snowflakes, no two no-hitters are the same—as I've learned over the years.

Of the 11 total no-hitters that I've seen, I've broadcast 10 of them. I was supposed to broadcast the 11th one. It occurred during my first big-league season in 1953. The TV station for which I was going to broadcast St. Louis Browns games did not have its tower erected yet. But I did get to watch Bobo Holloman pitch a no-hitter for the Browns against the Philadelphia A's. It was his first big-league start and he beat the A's, 6-0. He ended up 3-7 that year, made only 10 starts, and went back to the minors in 1954. He never made a trip back to the big leagues after pitching that season.

In 1955, I saw "Sad Sam" Jones—who was lucky enough to also be known as "Toothpick Sam"—pitch a no-hitter for the Cubs against the Pirates at Wrigley Field. He got his nicknames honestly, since he never smiled and constantly chewed toothpicks. Here he was pitching a no-hitter and leading 4-0 heading into the ninth inning. He walked the first three batters he faced that inning, and we all wondered whether Stan Hack, the manager, was going to take him out. Hack went out to the mound and said, "Sam, if you walk one more guy, I've got to take you out." Not only did Jones not walk anybody else, he struck out Dick Groat, Roberto Clemente, and Frank Thomas in order to wrap up the game. A mere 4,000 were at that game.

Flash forward to 1962, and I caught my third no-hitter as Bill Monbouquette of the Boston Red Sox threw a no-hitter against the Chicago White Sox. What makes the story interesting is that he was pitching against Early Wynn, who was going for his 300th career victory. At the age of 42, Wynn started that '62 season just eight wins shy of 300. He won seven in a hurry, but then hit a rut trying to win his eighth.

For the White Sox in those days, a big inning was when Luis Aparicio would lead off with a single, steal second, have Nellie Fox bunt him over to third, and then be knocked in when Sherm Lollar hit a sacrifice fly. The Sox would go way out in front, 1-0.

On August 1, Wynn was still stuck on 299 victories and facing a mediocre Red Sox team known as a "country club team." The Red Sox were partyers, including their manager, Pinky Higgins. So we thought Wynn was going to win that game against this club. Some of the Boston players told Wynn that if he'd taken better care

of himself, he'd have won his 300th a long time ago. His reply: "Yeah, but think of all the fun I would have missed." That was Early Wynn. He was the guy who said he'd throw at his mother if she was in the batter's box. He drove managers crazy, going 3-and-2 on every hitter. But that's the way he pitched. Then he'd get you out with a high fastball or a high slider.

The Sox were so convinced he was going to win No. 300 that night that they put on a big program commemorating his career, which began in 1939 and would stretch yet another year before he retired. In that game, though, Wynn got no run support. Monbouquette, who was 17 years younger than Wynn, pitched a no-hitter—and even had a hit himself against Wynn. The disappointment was crushing for Wynn, who didn't win another game the rest of the year. However, in 1963, the Cleveland Indians took him back. In July of '63, he lasted just five innings against the Kansas City A's before running out of gas and being removed. But he left with the lead—and earned his 300th win.

Spinning ahead to 1967, my fourth no-hitter was thrown by Don Wilson of the Astros, who no-hit the Braves in the Astrodome. To end the game, Wilson struck out Henry Aaron. It was almost like Wilson said, "Well, Hammer, if you're going to beat me and cost me this game, you're going to have to hit my heater." Leading 2-0, Wilson threw Aaron three straight fastballs—low, medium, and high—to strike him out and preserve the no-hitter. It was Wilson's 15th strikeout of the game against three walks.

Two years later, the Braves were on the wrong end of a no-hitter again, this time by Ken Holtzman of the Cubs. Holtzman was holding on to an early 3-0 lead heading into the seventh when Aaron hit a long ball to left field. Not only did it look like the no-hitter was gone, but the shutout, too. Aaron's hit look destined for the seats. My old pal Jack Brickhouse was doing the game on WGN television, and he blurted out, "There goes the no-hitter!" But there was a strong wind blowing in from Waveland Avenue— so strong that it blew the ball back into the field of play, allowing leftfielder Billy Williams to catch it with his back to the infield. After that, Holtzman settled down to wrap up the no-hit bid. This might have been the only no-hitter in which the pitcher failed to record at least one strikeout.

The Braves finally got a no-hitter in their favor in 1973 when knuckleballer Phil Niekro tossed one against the San Diego Padres in Atlanta. It was the only no-hitter Niekro ever pitched, though he won more than 300 games.

In 1976, my first year with the Pirates, I broadcast my seventh no-hitter, this one by Pirates pitcher John Candelaria at Three Rivers Stadium against the Dodgers. In that game, Danny Murtaugh, the Pirates manager, decided that since the Dodgers were throwing a lefty, he would use Bill Robinson, an outfielder, at third base. Prior to the 1976 season, Robinson had only played 14 games at third base—all in the 1973 season—and had committed a whopping three errors against just 10 assists. He had played third a little more frequently in 1976, but he was by no means an adequate fielder at that position.

In the third inning, Candelaria walked Steve Yeager with one out. Yeager was forced out at second on a ball hit by the pitcher, Doug Rau. With Rau on first, shortstop Frank Taveras made an error to allow Dave Lopes to reach base, putting runners on first and second. Robinson followed that up by committing an error on a ball hit by Ted Sizemore to load the bases with two outs. We thought that was going to cost Candelaria the shutout and possibly the no-hitter. But, to his credit, Candelaria was one of the top young pitchers at that time. He got Bill Russell to ground out to the shortstop to end the inning. Candelaria cruised the rest of the way, posting six straight 1-2-3 innings to notch the 2-0 victory.

It would be a full decade before my next no-hitter: the Mike Scott pennant-clinching no-hitter in 1986. My ninth came seven years later, in 1993. Darryl Kile beat the Mets, 7-1, in the Astrodome. Dallas Green, the manager of the Mets at the time and a guy who knew his baseball, told me that for nine innings, Kile was throwing the greatest curveball he had ever seen. Still, Kile lost the shutout when his best friend, Jeff Bagwell, made a throwing error. Even though he pitched a no-hitter, the Mets did score a run on the error. Kile finished the game with nine strikeouts and one walk.

Four years later, the Astros were on the short end of a no-hitter: a noteworthy 10-inning gem by Francisco Cordova and Ricardo Rincon of the Pirates. Nobody scored until the 10th, when the Pirates won it on a three-run, walk-off home run by pinch-hitter Mark Smith. It is the only extra-inning combined no-hitter in baseball history. Cordova threw nine innings, striking out 10 and walking two. But Rincon was credited with the win after working a scoreless.

The pinnacle of all my calls is probably Aaron's 715th home run. It's certainly the most unique of my calls, because a chance like that only comes around once every lifetime for an announcer—if he or she is extremely lucky. But a close second would be my calls of Nolan Ryan's first major-league strikeout and his 4,000th. His first, which came on September 11, 1966, was Braves pitcher Pat Jarvis; his 4,000th, which came on July 11, 1985, was Mets outfielder and former Astros teammate Danny Heep.

In one of the most impressive feats that I've been around to see, Ernie Banks hit five grand slams during the 1955 season, my first with the Cubs. I broadcast the fifth one. I was also on the air for Stan Musial's five homers in a 1954 doubleheader at Sportsman's Park in St. Louis. Eighteen years later, I was the broadcaster in Atlanta when Nate Colbert of the San Diego Padres duplicated Musial's feat to become the only other player in history to accomplish it.

One of my favorite calls came on the triple-play Atlanta made in 1969 against the Cubs. It happened in Atlanta-Fulton County Stadium on August 29 during the first inning. It's a lot to keep track of, but here we go: The inning began with a pair of singles by Cubs middle infielders Don Kessinger and Glenn Beckert. Pitching for the Braves was Pat Jarvis, and after allowing the two hits, he then balked. So, with Kessinger on third and Beckert on second and no outs in the inning, Billy Williams stepped to the plate.

With an 0-2 count, Williams hit a ground ball to Orlando Cepeda at first base. Cepeda stepped on the bag for the first out, then threw to shortstop Gil Garrido, who had slipped behind the runner at third. Kessinger was caught in a rundown between third and home that involved catcher Bob Didier, third baseman Clete Boyer, second baseman Felix Millan, and Jarvis. After several tosses, Millan finally tagged Kessinger near home plate for the second out. Beckert, the runner at second, was trying to make it to third but was caught in no-man's land between second and third. Millan fired the ball to leftfielder Rico Carty, who had sprinted in from the outfield to help out, and Carty tagged Beckert out at third.

It was not only the first triple-play in the history of the Atlanta Braves, but also a historic one because seven of the nine fielders were involved, which tied a major-league record. To me, that was a most unusual call, and it involved so many great players.

15

MY GREATEST GUESTS

will go to my deathbed insisting that longtime Chicago Cubs and White Sox broadcaster Bob Elson was the greatest interviewer ever. It didn't matter whether he was interviewing a politician, a movie star, or an athlete—he got the most out of his interviews. He taught me one important thing: to have some idea of what I wanted to discuss, but to never prepare questions ahead of time. The key to a good interview is for the interviewer to react to the interviewee.

My guests throughout the years have been varied, of course. Certain ones do stick out amongst the crowd. The manager I enjoyed talking with the most was former Pirates skipper Chuck Tanner, because he was so exuberant and easy to talk to. He was just a treasure to interview five days a week. As was former White Sox and Orioles manager Paul Richards. Richards could mesmerize an audience. When we'd go on road trips and the club wasn't doing that well or he wanted to show off, he'd have one of his coaches go to a grocery store and get sardines, bratwurst, liver sausage, and crackers. Then he'd have the bellman come in and fill the bathtub up with beer bottles on ice. I'll never forget the memories of those sessions where Richards would talk baseball. He could get a group of writers and broadcasters together and keep them spellbound.

I loved talking to Nellie Fox. He was a little chatterbox, so much fun to be around. I've interviewed Stan Musial at Old-Timers Games and gotten a kick out of him. He's very outgoing. Joe Torre was always a good interview when he was a player with the Braves. Nowadays, he's truly the most conversant of any manager, which might also be because he spent some years on the other side of the microphone as a broadcaster with the Angels.

Another of my all-time favorite interviewees was Pete Rose. Pete was always great to me, and as many times as I interviewed him over the years, that's surprising. He was always open to interviews. Since Pete was banned from baseball, I've remained in his corner. I just wanted him to say he was sorry. But he finally lost me with the ill timing of his book. I think that book hurt him. He was trying to persuade the nation that he ought to be granted induction into the Hall of Fame. But he never came out and said, "I made a mistake. I'm sorry." That's all he had to say.

Not everyone in baseball is cooperative, unfortunately. Former Astros manager Terry Collins, for example, reacted poorly to tough losses. If we lost a close game, he was often irked about one particular player whom he felt lost the game for us. He knew he was going to have to be interviewed by me, but when he saw me coming he kind of gave me a grimace. His body language was saying, "Do we have to do this?" He never turned me down, but maybe that's because he was getting paid to do it. Maybe that helped.

Sometimes in baseball, language can be a barrier preventing a broadcaster from doing a good interview. When I was with the Braves and I wanted to feature a Latino guest who didn't speak English very well, I used Rico Carty as my interpreter. That was fun because Rico got a kick out of it.

Milo interviews Pete Rose in 1980.

I don't interview players anymore so I don't get to know them as well as in the old days. But I make a point if a new guy's coming around to introduce myself and say hello. I'll say, "Boy, I really enjoyed your performance in the game the other night. I'm Milo Hamilton, the announcer for the Astros."

It never hurts to get off on the right foot. I guess that's something else that I've learned over the years.

16

PARTNER MAKES PERFECT

It makes logical sense: having a good partner makes me a better broadcaster. Since I'm a play-by-play man, I need to be coupled with a great analyst. And I need to have confidence in that person. He should be someone who makes me comfortable not only in the booth, but also when we're away from it—on the field, in the press dining room, or traveling from city to city.

In some booths, the play-by-play guy is considered the No. 1 guy; in others, it's the analyst. It just depends on who carries the bigger name, or who has more longevity. The No. 2 broadcaster needs to accept that role, and not try to push him- or herself into the spotlight. That's a no-win situation. As in show business, the second banana can't step on the toes of the lead actor. Booths are small spaces to begin with, so the broadcasters better be living in harmony.

I've discussed what it's like to work in a booth lacking harmony when I was in Chicago working with Harry Caray. But I also enjoyed some good times in the Windy City. In the middle innings of my broadcasts with Jack Brickhouse, I worked alongside Lou Boudreau. Lou was like a nice old pair of comfortable bedroom slippers. I slipped them on, put my feet up on the ottoman, and it was perfection.

Lou was a great guy and was beloved by his audience for his past accomplishments. But when he started in 1958, he wasn't a very good broadcaster. However, by the time I got there, Lou had really become a good analyst after working with Jack Quinlan and Vince Lloyd all those years. Then in 1983 and '84, I went over to radio only because it was apparent that I wasn't going to get anywhere with Harry Caray after working with him one year. I had Boudreau as my sidekick for those two seasons, and it was two of my most enjoyable years at the microphone.

When I arrived in Houston, however, things were shaky at the start. During spring training I worked with Gene Elston. We had worked together in Chicago so we had known each other for years. But I was the new guy on the block. Before we went on the air for our first broadcast, I said to Gene, "Tell me what kind of a role you want to play." And he said, "When you're here, your microphone will not be on. You will talk in the second half when I don't talk."

It was hardly a friendly welcome. But he was the lead announcer and had been in Houston for over 20 years, so there wasn't a hell of a lot I could say. Luckily, we only worked together during that spring training. During the regular season, Larry Dierker was part of the broadcast team. Gerry Trupiano, who is now with the Red Sox, was on the crew, too. Elston and I switched booths—swapping partners—every other day. One day, Elston would do radio and I'd do TV, and the next day we'd change booths altogether.

Then, after my second year in Houston, Elston was fired. That gave me the opportunity to work with Dierker more frequently, and he really became a terrific analyst. I nicknamed him "the Wrangler" because the first day I was in spring training in

Kissimmee in 1985, he was walking ahead of me after the game in a pair of Wrangler jeans. Across the back pocket was stitched the brand name, so I just said, "Hey, Wrangler, hold up." I started calling him Wrangler on the air then and it stuck—even the fans started calling him Wrangler.

But somewhere along the line, he thought radio was TV's stepchild, which is a mistake some broadcasters make. They think TV is "it," so they underplay their broadcast on the radio. His attitude changed, and it became noticeable to me, if not to the listener. I could tell a difference in the way he prepared for the games, and in the effort he put forth on the air.

So then when he was named manager, Vince Cotroneo, who had been our announcer in Triple-A, was brought in to be my new partner. I wasn't crazy about the decision, but I didn't fight it, either. Vince was—and still is—a talented announcer. But he blew his chance to become an elite broadcaster. He kept politicking to do more than the two innings he was hired to do. And my boss, Jamie Hildreth, made it abundantly clear to Vince that it was not going to happen. Every time Vince pleaded, Jamie would remind him that his assignment was to do two innings and provide color for Milo.

One time he called me on the phone out of the blue before spring training and asked, "How about this year I do three innings?" I replied, "I don't think so. You're doing the third and the seventh." I didn't hang up, but I left him with a clear impression that it wasn't going to happen. The straw that broke the camel's back was when his wife went to bat for him. A couple of the coaches' wives came to me, followed by the coaches, too. They all said, "You've got to do something about Vince Cotroneo." And I had no idea what they were going on about. Apparently, Vince's wife envisioned herself as a player's wife, sat with them at the games, and would blurt out, "Vince really ought to be doing the games. He's a lot better than Milo, and it's time that he did the games."

In the first place, the players' wives and the coaches' wives liked me, so they were open with me about her remarks. And so I confronted Vince about it and he denied it. I never issued an

Milo with partner Alan Ashby and engineer Mike "the Loose" Cannon as painted by artist Opie Otterstad.

ultimatum, but at the end of that year, it was time for him to go. I think he realized it, too, as he applied for and was given the color job with the Rangers.

That's when we brought Alan Ashby in full time, and he has grown into the position like topsy. That was nine years ago. He's a great analyst, and his play-by-play is damn good, too. Alan is just a great guy—period. And he's incredibly popular.

What impresses me most about Alan is his confidence and ability as an interviewer. Not all ballplayers are good interviewers, but Alan does an excellent job with his pre- and postgame interviews. Working with him is an ideal situation, and I hope that however long I'm here, he's in the booth with me.

Ashby does the fourth and seventh innings now.

The key to a successful broadcast is having good rapport between the announcers, and being comfortable with each other's roles. I don't ask my partner to do something he is uncomfortable with. I use him in the right role, as I did with Boudreau in Chicago; Dierker when he was in his prime; and Ashby, who is getting better every day. They have all fit like a glove.

17

BOOTHS—GOOD AND BAD

My office is the broadcast booth. And in my line of work, my office can change several times a week. Sometimes it's comfortable and spacious, sometimes it's small and cramped, and sometimes it's just an afterthought nearly forgotten by the ballpark planners.

Many of the booths of old were tiny, added to the ballpark after the park had been built. They built them up high, far from the action on the field. But there were exceptions, like Tiger Stadium and Ebbets Field. You weren't *up* in the press box, you were *down*— you could almost reach out and touch the third-base coach. There was almost as much chance of chatter from the field interfering with your broadcast as chatter from the stands. The broadcast booth at Tiger Stadium was located down in a well, and there was no bathroom. At Ebbets Field, the booth was situated in a little gondola. It wasn't a great vantage point to call the balls and strikes because the broadcaster sat just 100 feet away from the plate.

But those booths were charming nonetheless. When I first arrived in Pittsburgh in 1976, the booth in Forbes Field was clear in the upper deck on top of the ladies restroom. Flushing toilets became a part of our surrounding crowd noise. They eventually moved the booth down to the press level, but the ceilings were so low, I had to be careful not to conk my head.

D.C. Stadium—now known as RFK—was even worse. When they opened it for the second edition of the Senators, they completely forgot about the broadcast booths. So they hung them under the upper deck with hardly any head space. I was working with Bob Elson at that time. He walked in, hit his head on the beam, and collapsed like he'd been shot. I'm the only active broadcaster to have worked in both the old Griffith Stadium and the current RFK Stadium, which was known as D.C. Stadium when it first opened.

The Yankee Stadium booth is fine now. But the broadcast booths were exposed to the elements in the old Yankee Stadium. If it rained, the broadcasters were in the rain. The booths were located right on the edge of the mezzanine and there you were. The fans were in your back. It was a refreshing change to find a new booth in Yankee Stadium in 2003.

I prefer an enclosed booth, especially since the summer weather can often be wild and unpredictable. I've experienced some dangerous weather conditions. I don't like it when lightning pops around the park, there's heavy rain, and the wind blows in and ruins your scorecard or some of your record books. Some of the new booths haven't guarded against that.

When they built the new press box at Wrigley, they made the WGN booth large at the expense of the visiting radio booth. It's so small that if my partner needs to exit the booth, I've got to get up, too, and leave the booth to allow him to exit. The engineer has no room at all. And that's a relatively *new* booth.

A second poor booth was built by another one of my former employers, the Atlanta Braves. When they built the Olympic Stadium in Atlanta and then put the Braves in it, they paid no mind

Milo's view from the radio booth at Minute Maid Park. *Stephen P. O'Brien*

to the visiting radio booth. Trying to squeeze two announcers into the booth is like forcing them to become Siamese twins. The engineer can't see the game. And the thing that bothers me most is, they designed the booth that way on the *recommendation* of the Braves announcers. I'm not asking for the world. Just give us some courtesy, some comfort, and some space.

The booths at the new parks in Philadelphia and San Francisco are ideal. But there's no excuse for Pittsburgh's booth, especially since it's another new park. PNC Park is a beautiful ballpark. I love the scenery, I love the river, and I love the bridge that the fans cross to get to the stadium. For some unknown reason, however, they put the press box and the broadcast booth halfway to the moon. You cannot even read the numbers on the uniforms from the booth without the aid of binoculars.

I've asked Dick Freeman, who was president of the Pirates when they built it, why they built it that way. He said they placed the booth there because they felt they needed the seats. I said, "Have you looked out there lately? You could have built it down under a lower deck and had a nice press box and nice broadcast booth." If you're designing a ballpark and you don't know where to place a broadcast booth, how about asking?

That's what they did when they built the new park in Houston, and the booths turned out to be very nice. They're all about the same size, so there's no favoritism for visiting or home broadcasters. And that's the way it ought to be.

I've broadcast games in 51 different big-league parks—some old, some new, and some that combined 21st-century amenities with 20th-century traditions. I have to work in whatever broadcast booth they give me. In that way, my office is hardly ideal, even if some fans might argue that I've got the best seat in the house.

18

A CHANGING GAME

The advent of free agency in baseball is the biggest change I've seen during my career. It totally changed the game, shifting the power balance away from the owners and toward the players. But there was little common sense used when instituting free agency. While it worked out well for current players, old-time players weren't given their proper due. A proper pension fund wasn't established to take care of those old players, and when hospital bills began to rack up debt, it left their wives penniless.

But free agency is old news now. One of today's hot-button topics is expansion—or rather, contraction. I'm not certain if eliminating the Minnesota Twins or any other franchise is going to solve any of baseball's problems. But I know that some people in baseball are hoping that specific clubs fail because it justifies their opinion: that baseball has expanded beyond its means. I do generally think that eliminating four teams would probably be in the game's best interest. Major League Baseball expanded way too fast and set franchises up to fail by placing them in poor baseball markets. I don't think they did enough homework on each city before making a decision.

They had no reason to put a team in Tampa, for example. South Florida didn't have much of a track record with the Marlins. Now, baseball has got two cities in a fixed-income state. There aren't a lot of people there who can afford to support baseball: just look at the attendance for proof. The Marlins did well when they were in the World Series, but a team cannot be counted on to win big every year.

Baseball has to make up its mind and stop going back and forth. It can't keep Montreal afloat while it relocates, bails out Jerry Colangelo in Arizona after he overinflated his payroll en route to winning the World Series, and then choose to ignore other teams that are in dire straits.

One of the problems in eliminating any team, of course, is getting the players association to agree to terms. It wouldn't allow commissioner Bud Selig to get rid of the designated hitter. If the union were willing to put its foot down regarding a change that would affect a handful of players' standing in the games, then it will most definitely put its foot down when it comes to the removal of an entire team—or two. But as the old argument goes: Shouldn't the commissioner be the commissioner for everybody and not just the owners?

As tough as the automotive union was against Ford or General Motors, when push came to shove, the union people had enough sense to know that jobs are what they are fighting for. They knew that if they pushed too far and the jobs disappeared, then they have failed as a union. I don't ever get the feeling that Donald Fehr, who heads up the players union, and his people have the same love of the players and are looking out for the betterment of their lives and that of the game. Both sides need to find some common ground. It can't be all take and no give.

Most fans are pretty discerning. They know baseball is a game of ups and downs, a game of streaks. And they accept that because history tells them that it's part of the game. But fans have a hard time understanding the work stoppages that we've endured over the years. The worst was the cancellation of the World Series, which happened during the strike of 1994-'95.

I think we've bounced back from that strike. But I still wonder whether the strike could have been prevented. Can you stop something that caused such a loggerhead between two parties? The owners were trying to bust the players union and it seemed like the union was trying to bust the owners. Thank goodness we had Mark McGwire, Sammy Sosa, and Cal Ripken to help restore fan interest in the game.

When the Basic Agreement expires after the 2006 season, we could be in serious trouble once again. Major League Baseball will ask Fehr, "Do you want 80 percent of something or 100 percent of nothing? If you carry us to the brink again, it's going to be 100 percent of nothing." In that situation, Fehr will have to not only consider the livelihood of the players and their families, but also that of the thousands of people who are employed by ballclubs in some capacity. The players association will need to be willing to give up something, even if it means sacrificing the DH rule. The owners might then choose to increase the rosters to 26, creating more jobs. That would be a good compromise.

There's little solidarity in baseball. If there's one thing that sets former NFL commissioner Pete Rozelle apart from all the other commissioners—regardless of sport—it would be his ability to unite a league. He did that when he brought the AFL and NFL together. But Rozelle also brought the *owners* together. He got them all on the same page. It's a rare day when one NFL owner criticizes another NFL owner, but baseball owners do it all the time.

NFL teams also share television revenue. Because of individual cable-TV contracts, sometimes you think that it's the New York Yankees and 29 other teams. They get so much money from television—it puts them at an incredibly unfair advantage. George Steinbrenner probably has more TV money in the bank before he goes to spring training than other clubs make from all their sources combined during the rest of the season. His ticket sales are just gravy.

Why don't the owners, instead of bickering and badgering and insulting each other, use some common sense and take steps to level the playing field? Impose a salary cap or whatever. Just do *something*.

Bud Selig had to do something after the 2002 All-Star Game ended in a 7-7 tie. Selig would have made more friends if he would have said, "Let's finish this game." Instead, he opened a Pandora's box for the national media, allowing them to say, "The All-Star Game has to be more meaningful." The next year, he decided to award home-field advantage in the World Series to the league that wins the All-Star Game.

That wasn't the right decision on Selig's part because he created a situation where a team that won more regular-season games but happened to be in the league that lost the All-Star Game would be penalized in the World Series. It's the old story: you can't fix a 17-inch gash with a one-inch Band-Aid.

The starting times of games are also beginning to become ridiculous. National TV seems to be calling the shots on when games start. But it's a shame that some of these games—even during the playoffs—start so late that baseball fans young *and* old have to go to bed before the National Anthem is sung. What's wrong with a few afternoon baseball games? I remember when it was *all* day games. Most fans still found a way to listen to the game.

The whole thing boils down to one word: greed. Baseball commands more money for games played during prime-time television. But that doesn't make it right. Are you going to tell me that there are more people watching a baseball game during the 11 o'clock hour than there would have been if the game would have been played earlier in the evening, or at one o'clock in the afternoon?

While we're on the subject of scheduling, let's talk about interleague play as well. I don't like it, because just as with game-time scheduling, revenue sharing, or expansion, those making the decisions aren't utilizing much common sense. Do the White Sox-Cubs, Yankees-Mets, Dodgers-Angels, A's-Giants, or even Rangers-Astros make sense? Sure they do, for obvious reasons. But there are so many other matchups that are simply meaningless. In 2005, the

Astros headed to Toronto and Baltimore, and Tampa Bay visited Houston. These were games that didn't draw flies. For the few interesting series during interleague play, there are just as many boring ones to balance things out.

Maybe someday soon we'll see these crazy salaries start to come back down to Earth. The contract that Alex Rodriguez signed for $252 million certainly didn't do the Texas Rangers any favors. They finished last in their division each of three years he was with them—even though he won the MVP in 2003. Rodriguez was actually awarded a bonus for winning the MVP. Why would an owner ever allow a bonus clause for a player who is already earning 25 million dollars a season? If you paid him that much, wasn't he *supposed* to win the MVP?

There are plenty of factors that work against smart economics in baseball. I don't respect those agents who are only interested in outdoing other agents. I don't believe in arbitration—one of the worst things to ever happen to the game—because it forces salaries to go up way too soon. If a ballclub offers $2 million and the player wants $5 million, the arbitrator has to choose one of the two. He can't negotiate a settlement. And worse yet: the arbitrators don't know much about baseball.

In addition, I don't believe in guaranteed contracts. I think there are so many potential concerns that enter into long-term contracts. Look at the guys who are making millions who get hurt and miss half a season or longer. How does the ballclub justify guaranteeing a contract to themselves, their auditors, and their other players? The A-Rod contract was out of whack from the start. It wasn't like the Rangers barely outbid somebody else for his services. The nearest bid from another team was $100 million less. If you knew that you could sign Rodriguez for $152 million, why would you give him $252 million?

The big salaries in baseball have widened the rift between players and fans. In this day and age of the sports talk show, it becomes a constant harangue. People call in and say, "He isn't worth that kind of money, and I'm never going to go see another game." Some people don't even give it a second thought. They want to go to the ballgame, and they don't care if the guy in the batter's box is making $5 million or $10 million a season. But for many fans, a player's salary becomes an issue. It promotes stories in the newspapers and in the periodicals, and it has a mushrooming effect.

I haven't had a lot of negotiations in my life on my baseball contracts. I've had managers through the years who negotiated my commercial fees and speaking engagements and things like that. But my baseball contracts I handled on my own, because I felt I knew more about my worth than any agent or manager could. And I never made any outlandish demands for raises because I've made a good living. But I also know that if I had been too demanding, there would have been some times when my employer would have said, "Milo, you've done a great job for us, but we think we might go in another direction." It never came to that.

Sometimes when I was getting ready to sign a new contract, I'd ask for something here or there. The team would come back with this or that and we would have a meeting of the minds—we were *open* to having a meeting of the minds. The owners and the players union historically have not been open to such meetings.

Hank Aaron's top salary was around $250,000, but the *minimum* salary today is more than $300,000. Joe DiMaggio had a great response to today's escalating salaries. A reporter asked him, "What would you say at contract time if you were playing now?" Joe replied, "I'd go to the owner, reach out my hand, and say, 'How you doin' today, partner?' I'd own part of the club."

Don't get me wrong. There was a time for Marvin Miller to come along. And I understood why the players union and free agency were needed; the owners did have it their way for a long time. Stan Musial and Joe DiMaggio had to battle for more money. Sandy Koufax and Don Drysdale had to stage a joint holdout to get what they felt they were worth. Some great players had to fight for good contracts. The balance had tilted too far the owners' way. But now it's gone too far in the players' direction. Some of the blame, however, rests on the owners' shoulders for not standing pat.

Now we're in the era of special demands, when a player will put clauses in his contract that provide him with special treatment. When Kevin Brown signed a seven-year contract for $105 million dollars, his contract included all sorts of specific perks. It really was ridiculous. But the Roger Clemens situation was different. Before he came out of retirement to sign with the Astros in 2004, Clemens went to Jeff Bagwell and Craig Biggio and told them that he was not always going to travel with the team. He asked if that bothered them and they gave him their blessing. The rest of the players agreed: if Bagwell and Biggio thought it was all right, then it was fine with them, too.

Clemens never flaunted his privileges or made unjust demands. And it wasn't like he was just showing up on his day to pitch—he got his work in, supported his teammates, and was a positive veteran role model. The fact that he wasn't with the team every day didn't bother me. Everyone from the owner on down to the manager and the players didn't have a problem with the treatment he received—and neither did the fans. Obviously, it worked out well for Houston: Clemens won the Cy Young award in 2004 and pitched the Astros into the playoffs for two straight seasons.

But we wouldn't have made the playoffs if not for one of baseball's positive changes. When the wild card was first introduced, I didn't like it. But after having time to see its impact on the game, I think it has been a good addition. Witness the World Series winners that have come from the wild-card spot in either league. The wild-card race maintains interest down the stretch, when a lot of clubs might not draw well if not for the wild-card situation. Of course, the Astros have benefited mightily. They were nearly out of the race in the middle of August in 2004. But the team kept drawing those huge crowds at the ballpark, and the team rallied to capture the wild card. So the wild card is one change that I'm okay with.

19

PLAYING COMMISSIONER

Hanging around baseball for six decades has given me a chance to see virtually every commissioner in action. My career spans every one of them, with the exception of Judge Kenesaw Mountain Landis. Happy Chandler has a great legacy. As much credit as Branch Rickey gets for integration and bringing in Jackie Robinson, Chandler's got to be right there with equal credit. He was commissioner when Jackie broke into the major leagues and when I began my baseball broadcasting career.

Chandler supported Rickey's decision, and even threatened to suspend players who were going to protest. There was some outcry, and some of the players from the South said they wouldn't play. The Phillies, under Ben Chapman, were talking about a boycott. But Happy said, "You'll play." If he'd have backed off from that, it would have had a long-lasting, damaging impact. I was surprised when Chandler was fired because he was such a gregarious, likeable guy. I thought he was a popular commissioner.

I didn't know Chandler's replacement, Ford Frick, all that well. He was a very quiet man, especially for a guy who was in the media business. He was a former sportswriter who once served as a ghostwriter for Babe Ruth. I thought he was a good commissioner. I don't remember anything that he did that would make me say, "Boy, I'm glad they got rid of him."

Frick's only downfall was that he was too close to Ruth. Do you think that if he hadn't been Ruth's ghostwriter that he would have decided to place an asterisk in the record books next to Roger Maris's 61 home runs? I sure don't.

Frick ushered baseball through its growth westward in 1958 and its first expansion in the modern era in 1960-'61. I thought it was time for the league to grow from 16 to 20 teams. The country was so much bigger, and it was time to reflect that growth in the major leagues. When I got in the game, there were only eight teams in each league, and there was nothing west of St. Louis. Then the Dodgers and Giants headed to the west coast and the game truly became the entire nation's pastime. The expansion in the early '60s filled a void, especially in New York, where two National League teams had departed, leaving only the Yankees. Even though the Mets were horrible, New York City fans didn't care. They just wanted another team to root for.

As for Spike Eckert, it's enough to say that the biggest fault of his being the commissioner was that he was elected in the first place. But I liked his replacement, Bowie Kuhn, a lot. I thought he was a standup guy who believed in the game. Kuhn was a batboy at old Griffith Stadium for the Washington Senators, and he must have had baseball in his blood. I appreciated him for his legal background, too. If he only would have stood his ground on the arbitration request, the game would be a lot different now.

I liked Peter Ueberroth as well. It's too bad that the one thing that he'll be remembered for is collusion. He rallied the owners together and said, "We've got to do something about holding the line on salaries." It ended up costing the owners millions in the end when they were found guilty of collusion. Ueberroth's message was not one of evil intent, though. All he was trying to say was, "We need to start showing some common sense on these salaries that are getting out of hand."

Bart Giamatti didn't last very long as commissioner. Being a huge fan of baseball, it must have really torn him apart to suspend Pete Rose. In his mind, though, he realized that he had to do it. But it was obvious how much Giamatti loved the game. If he had lived, I think he would have been a great commissioner.

I thought Fay Vincent might have been one of the most qualified of all the commissioners. But that may have cost him, because the owners didn't want a guy who was so qualified to be in charge. They ran him off. I was able to interview Vincent, and I was around him more than any of the other commissioners except Bowie Kuhn. Vincent was commissioner when I was elected into the Hall of Fame.

Current Major League Baseball commissioner Bud Selig knows that I don't agree with him on a lot of things. I've been on talk shows and I've said some things that have made their way back to him. I can tell by the way that he occasionally reacts when we're together. It's not what he says, but rather his body language. I've never muttered any cross words about Bud being a bad commissioner. I think he's done some good things, like the wild card. But he's not perfect. I'm not either, but that doesn't mean that I don't have my opinions about what I would do if I were commissioner.

First things first, I would do away with the designated hitter rule and arbitration. Then I would do something about the umpiring. I think umpiring in general has gone south over the years. All an umpire has to do is look in the rule book and there's a diagram of the strike zone. When is the last time you saw a game called according to that diagram?

If a pitch isn't between the belly-button and a little above your knees, it's not a strike. And I think Selig had the perfect opportunity to drive his memorandum home, by telling the umpires, "You will start calling the balls and strikes by the rule book." When Bruce Froemming replied, "I can't do that, I've got my own strike zone," the commissioner could have sent a clear message to every other umpire by saying, "Mr. Froemming, we don't need your services any longer."

I'd also like to see baseball get rid of this "warning" that is issued when a pitcher supposedly intentionally throws at a hitter. Are the umpires capable of reading a pitcher's mind to find out if he threw at a guy intentionally? The last time I checked, umpires don't have psychic powers. For years, the players took care of business pretty well without the umpire's help.

Another thing: try to speed up the game. Every spring training we hear about how they're going to speed things up. But there's never any noticeable improvement. If you're in that batter's box and you tell the pitcher to pitch, he should hurry up and pitch. Likewise, if the batter steps out without a good reason, no matter where the pitch is thrown, it should be called a strike. You could cut 20 minutes off every game by disciplining the batters who step in and out of the batter's box or the pitchers who dawdle on the mound.

Also, why are all of these visits to the mound so necessary? You've got a catcher out there who's running a lot of the game. If the manager comes out, and it's his second visit, you know the pitcher's gone. The minute he leaves that dugout, the umpire should say, "Whom do you want?" and point to the pen.

There's nothing we can do about the two-minute commercial breaks. That's a part of the economy of the game. And obviously there's nothing we can do when they add time to the commercials during the playoffs. There's so much money involved in the broadcast, but that simply places more emphasis on speeding up the game itself. The old games at the Polo Grounds and Ebbets Field often were over in one hour and 35 minutes. How many two-hour games have you seen in the last 10 years, though?

I'd change the Hall of Fame voting as well. Some of the guys who vote for the Hall of Fame haven't been in or around the game for two or more decades and don't see a lot of games. I'd make certain that those who are voting are still actively participating in the coverage of the game.

20

THE STEROIDS STENCH

The current commissioner's biggest challenge is dealing with the steroids controversy, which has turned into a bit of a crisis. It leaves a big question mark hanging over many prominent current and former players and the records that they set.

I have never seen anything questionable in a locker room, and I have never been in a trainer's room. I have seen people with suddenly larger bodies and wondered how they achieved such a transformation. But I can't say that I saw anything with my own two eyes. I still believe, however, that where there's smoke, there's fire. Nearly everyone denies using steroids. Even in his interview on *60 Minutes*, Jose Canseco qualified his responses with "maybe" or "sometimes." To his credit, Mike Wallace, the host, pinned him on all of it.

Baseball is headed in the right direction with the new anti-drug program they initiated in 2005, but I don't think that the penalties are strong enough. Although Bud Selig deserves credit for advocating a tougher drug enforcement plan after the 2005 World Series, I'd still like to see baseball take after the Olympics, where it's a two-year ban for the first offense. In baseball, it will take a while before an offender really gets hit between the eyes with a huge penalty. But maybe just having a policy in place will scare a good number of players from using steroids. Still, in my line of work, we worry that somebody will figure out a way to get ahead of the curve and fool the drug test.

If money and fame are what prompted these players to take steroids in the first place, then maybe baseball should now threaten them by voiding contracts and suspending careers. A guy may think, "I worked my butt off to get to the major leagues. Do I want to kiss all of that goodbye because I stuck something in my arm?"

We already lost Ken Caminiti. He became his own worst enemy, even though everyone was trying to help him. In the end, he turned on the people who reached out to him the most, and even alienated Jeff Bagwell and Craig Biggio, who stuck up for him through thick and thin. Caminiti was such a tragic case. I never had any idea anything was going on with him when he was in Houston. We started to hear stories about his problems with steroids while he was in San Diego, because some in the Padres organization began to openly address the problem.

The tragedy was that he was a gifted athlete, and yet he felt he still needed another edge. With his sort of ability, why was it necessary for him to further augment his natural talent? When he died at the age of 41, he left behind his wife, Nancy, who was a saint, and three lovely daughters. They're the ones now who have to deal with the painful memories.

Barry Bonds is an interesting study, too. I admire him as a player. His records speak for themselves. All of the MVPs that he has won surely put him in a class all by himself. Yet over recent years, there have been plenty of red flags in the case of Bonds. His supporters continue to note: innocent until proven guilty. Bonds has certainly made an ambitious attempt to appear innocent, to cover all the bases. Now we know that he has supposedly taken steroids—allegedly unbeknownst to him. My interpretation of everything I've read and heard is that it's almost like Bonds knows that some day the truth is going to come out.

I'm concerned about what's going to happen when and if he finally passes Hank Aaron's home run record; is there an asterisk in Bonds's future? I have mixed feelings about Bonds breaking Aaron's record because of my history with the Aaron home run. Henry probably put it in the best perspective when he said records are made to be broken; I guess that was the political and polite thing for Henry to say. Maybe secretly he thought that if Barry falls short, that would be all right too. But it's going to be interesting to see how baseball handles it, both when it happens and if it comes out—down the road—that he was on steroids for a significant amount of time. Will Major League Baseball permit his home run record to stand?

These concerns could also apply to Mark McGwire and Sammy Sosa. Jason Giambi wasn't in on any record chases, but he was an MVP and hit a lot of home runs. It taints his career, too, just as it does with Rafael Palmeiro's career. If Ford Frick could put an asterisk next to Roger Maris's name because he played in eight more games than Babe Ruth, are there enough asterisks to go around for Bonds, McGwire, and Sosa? The entire steriods mess sure makes the records of Roger Maris, Hank Aaron, and others look even more impressive.

Players know upfront that using steroids can potentially take years off of their lives. I guess the almighty dollar just jumps up and bites them. But I would hope that today—with all of the bad publicity and penalties involved with being caught—that a player taking steroids would have to say to himself, "What in the hell am I doing?"

At any rate, taking steroids is not fair to the guys who play it straight. It's not good for the game of baseball, and it's not good for the player as a person, either. Look no further than Caminiti for the proof.

21

MY DREAM TEAM

I haven't a clue precisely how many major league ballplayers I've seen over the years, but I do have a good grasp of which ballplayers I feel were the best at their positions. I won't limit my selections to players on the teams that I've worked for; instead, I'll just choose the best guys I've seen play with my own two eyes, from the past six decades.

At catcher, I'll take a guy who I feel reinvented the art of catching, to a degree. Johnny Bench caught one-handed—which was rare for a catcher in his time—and was a master at throwing out basestealers. He controlled a game from behind the plate and was rewarded for his efforts by winning 10 straight Gold Gloves and being named an All-Star 14 times. He was also Rookie of the Year in 1968 and twice won the NL MVP award. At the plate, he could hit a little, too. Bench clubbed 20 or more homers in 11 seasons, and twice knocked 40 or more out of the park. If I'm building a team, I'm starting with Bench.

Of the players whom I saw at first base, Willie Stargell and Willie McCovey were the best. Neither guy was a slouch at the plate, but I'd probably give "Stretch" the slight nod over "Pops." Mark McGwire was a great-hitting first baseman, too, but he wasn't as good with the big claw as either Stargell or McCovey. I'd actually rank Gil Hodges in third, ahead of McGwire. I have a vote on the Old Timers Committee for the Hall of Fame and vote for Hodges every time. In terms of personality and character, he was one of my favorites. Hodges was just a great guy to be around. But for what he did on the field, I'd have to take McCovey as my first baseman. Stargell can be my left-handed pinch-hitter extraordinaire.

My second baseman probably won't come as a surprise: Ryne Sandberg. The popular pick, and with good reason, is Rogers Hornsby. To me, he's the greatest righthanded hitter in the history of the game: anybody who hits .400 three times his career and twice wins the Triple Crown has to be considered in that light. Over a six-year span in the 1920s, Hornsby hit .370, .397, .401, .384, .424, and .403 to win the batting title six years in a row. I got to know him because he used to come to Wrigley Field a lot in the '50s. And in my first television game with the Browns, I had the difficult task of interviewing him. But I can't choose him for my team since I didn't see him on the field as a player. I did see Bill Mazeroski, who was the greatest second baseman making the double-play. I swear the ball never touched Maz's glove when he was the middle man on the double-play. But I'm sticking with Hall of Famer "Ryno" for his Gold Gloves and his power.

I'll fill out the rest of the infield with Luis Aparicio at shortstop and Brooks Robinson at third base. Aparicio gets the nod over Ernie Banks because Banks also played a lot of first base late in his career. Luis was a Gold-Glove shortstop his entire career and a great base-stealer who led the league in stolen bases nine consecutive seasons. Robinson gets the call at third over Eddie Mathews, power hitter and solid fielder, and Mike Schmidt, another home-run hitter who was quite good with the glove.

Robinson was simply in a world of his own. He had the advantage of playing in several World Series at the height of his career—so his spectacular plays often came in the game's brightest spotlight. He did things on the field that should not have been possible. And Brooksie was a good hitter, too.

I'll make a controversial call for my outfield and select Mickey Mantle to play centerfield. Mantle's defense is often overlooked. He made it look so easy in the field, gliding to the ball with grace. I'll admit that choosing between Mantle and Willie Mays in center is a tough call for me. Willie hit more home runs in his career, but he also enjoyed a career with fewer injuries. My source for how great Mantle was is his former manager, Casey Stengel. Stengel felt that if Mantle had played on two good legs, he might have been the greatest player of all time. He was the complete package: power, speed, defense. When he was healthy, he could have stolen 40-50 bases in a season. But on those talented Yankees clubs, he didn't need to. Under the Stengel regime, stealing bases wasn't required or encouraged. Mantle would crush a long home run, and the next day he would drop down a bunt. On two good knees, he was one of the fastest guys ever timed running down the line from the left side of the plate. In the other corner outfield spots, I'll take Hammerin' Hank Aaron and put him in left and have Roberto Clemente in right.

I'll go with a four-man pitching rotation, as all of my starters are workhorses. I'll take a pair of lefties and a pair of righties. From the left side, I'm going with a pair of polar opposites: Warren Spahn and Sandy Koufax. Spahn was a crafty pitcher, whereas Koufax was just plain dominating. Spahn won 20 or more games 13 times in his career, which spanned 21 seasons. Koufax's career was cut short due to an arm injury, but for six seasons he was the most dominating pitcher in the game—maybe ever. Speaking of dominating, if I had to choose anyone to start the seventh game of the World Series, I'd select Bob Gibson. Gibby completed eight of the nine games he started in the World Series, won seven of those games, and posted a 1.89 ERA. And who can forget Tom Seaver? I'll take him for my final rotation slot. He was very methodical and able to set guys up better than anybody I ever saw. Plus he was in my induction class at Cooperstown.

In the pen I'll take two guys who get unfairly ignored by the Hall of Fame voters: Goose Gossage and Bruce Sutter. Gossage often worked more than one inning, and Sutter was the guy who really brought the true splitter to the major leagues. There were some years where Sutter seemed like he was unhittable, both with the Cubs and Cardinals. These two guys were two of the absolute best in the business.

To keep all of these Hall of Famers in check, I'll go with former Indians and White Sox skipper Al Lopez, another Hall of Famer. Lopez, who passed away at the age of 97 right after the 2005 World Series, was a tough-minded silent type who earned his players' respect, was exceptional at controlling the umpires, and was also good with a deck of cards in his hand. He'll need some help on the bench, so I'll take Chuck Tanner, who was a great favorite of mine because he was so optimistic and expressive. And to round out the bench, I'll save a spot for Eddie Stanky. I was only with Stanky for one year in St. Louis, but he left a lasting impression on me. Even the players who didn't like him would tell you that as far as strategy and thinking ahead were concerned, Stanky might have been as good as anyone who ever managed. Boy, could he manage.

That's my team, and I'll take them in a seven-game series against anyone else's group of guys.

Every great team needs an outstanding general manager, and Gerry Hunsicker fills the bill for me. Gerry did a terrific job for the Astros for a decade, plus, he's a treasured friend.

The most unappreciated member of a Major League team is the traveling secreary. For 20 years, Barry Waters has served the Astros in this capacity. His devotion for me personally is beyond description, but calling 9-1-1 on the road and arranging ambulances should give you an idea. For my dream team, Waters is a sure bet.

Finally, the Astros equipment manager, Dennis Liborio, is the most beloved man in his profession. "Gallagher," as he's known around the Astros, received the Long and Meritorious Service Award at the Houston Baseball Dinner, and that speaks volumes. He rounds out a truly spectacular team.

22

AWAY FROM THE DIAMOND

During my 60 years at the microphone, I've covered a lot more than baseball. In the early years, I announced a lot of Golden Glove fights at the high school field house in Moline, Illinois. They would cram about 6,000 people into the gymnasium, and the bout's winners went on to the National finals that were held at the Chicago Stadium. During my time in and around Iowa in the late '40s and early '50s, I also broadcast University of Iowa football and basketball games.

When I wasn't on the gridiron, I was on the golf course. I did a lot of golf tournaments, like the Illinois Amateur tournament, which was held at the Short Hills Country Club in East Moline, Illinois, and the Western Open, which came to Davenport, Iowa. The Western Open provided my first opportunity to broadcast on a national radio network. At that time, we only broadcast the final three holes, as there wasn't time to broadcast all 18. There I was near the green, whispering into the microphone so as not to disturb the golfers.

My folks were listening to the tournament from their home along with my entire hometown, and I was excited to know that my voice was going out around the country. After the 18th hole, I walked toward the press tent glowing with satisfaction. "Oh boy, you lucky son of a gun," I said to myself. "You were just heard all over the country." I arrived at the press tent and discovered that there had been a power failure for 45 minutes, and no one—except me—had heard the broadcast. Nobody on the crew had the sense to come out and tell me. Imagine the sinking feeling! I thought I had done a pretty good job, with network exposure, but instead I was talking to myself.

In addition to broadcasting football games of my alma mater, I also did Northwestern football in the early '60s while I was in Chicago. In Atlanta, I did some Georgia Tech games in 1972 and then three years of Ohio State games on television from 1969-1971. But after 1972, I took some time off to focus solely on baseball. I was tired of hopping flights and spending more time at the airport than at home.

I have also broadcast basketball games off and on from 1950-1992. In the early '50s I broadcast some Iowa basketball games, and while I was in Chicago working for the White Sox I announced games for the Chicago Zephyrs of the NBA, Ray Meyer's DePaul teams, and the Northwestern Wildcats. When I moved to Atlanta, I did a season's worth of Georgia Tech basketball games, and then upon moving back to Chicago in 1980 I did more DePaul games as well as the Chicago Bulls. My move to Houston allowed me to broadcast Southwest Conference basketball games, and during the 1991-'92 season, I filled in with the Houston Rockets. When I was inducted into the Hall of Fame in 1992, my color analyst on Southwest Conference broadcasts was Guy V. Lewis, the famous coach of the "Phi Slamma Jamma" University of Houston Cougars. He belongs in the Basketball Hall of Fame.

All in all, 25 years of football and 40 years of basketball—in addition to over 50 years of baseball coverage—made for a full and rewarding broadcasting career.

From reading this book, you may have assumed that the love of my life is baseball. But in truth, for more than half a century, the love of my life was my wife, Arlene. I met her only a year after becoming a professional baseball announcer. The year was 1951, and I was doing some high school football games on the side. I met Arlene Weiskopf through the Davenport High School football coach, Butch Stofa. She was Butch's secretary at the time.

I went to visit Butch at his office one day because I was missing some advance information on the upcoming game that he was supposed to pass on to me. During my visit with Butch, I was introduced to Arlene. As I left the offices, I stopped at a drinking fountain that was located near Arlene's desk. I looked at her long enough to know that she registered my glance. On the way to the car, I said to my co-worker, who was there with me, "You know that girl, Butch's secretary? I'm going to marry her."

I had never seen her in my life. But a few days later, I called her and asked her out on a date. She said she was busy. I found out later that she really just wanted to find out more about me from Butch. He admitted to her that he had purposefully not given me the information so that I would visit him. He wanted any excuse to try to get Arlene and me together. That son of a gun was playing Cupid. Arlene told Butch that she didn't want to go out with some dumb sports announcer. She grew up in a rural area, and so she didn't know what the hell a sports announcer actually did.

But I didn't give up on Arlene. A few days after she turned me down I called back. I told her I was doing the Davenport game that Friday night, and I invited her to sit up in the booth and hear the broadcast. I mentioned that there was a big-band dance going on at the coliseum in Davenport after the game and suggested that we could go to the dance. This time, she accepted.

Then I asked her if she wanted to get dinner with me on Saturday night—but she declined. Not taking no for an answer, I said, "Well, what about Sunday night? My roommates and I are going to the game. We can all go together, and then afterwards we'll get some dinner, come back to my house, put on some records, and dance." She must have figured there was safety in numbers, since that would be our second date and two other

Milo wed the former Arlene Weiskopf in 1952.

couples would be there. We had a fabulous time, and as I took her home, I asked her to marry me. It was only our second date, but she said yes.

That was on a Sunday, and the next night I picked her up at work and we had dinner at the Sportsman's Grill. She said, "I don't want to go back to the apartment tonight, I want to go home to the farm and tell my mother." So we went to her parents' farm where she'd grown up. I dropped her off and left. She walked into her parents' bedroom and said, "Mother, I need to talk to you." And her mother said, "You're getting married, aren't you?"

Then they started making plans. A couple months later—on Thanksgiving weekend—we went to visit my parents in Fairfield, and I gave her a ring. We got married on April 6, 1952. I couldn't rub two quarters together and she had $175 in her bank account. Our honeymoon came months later, when I went to spring training. The radio station manager told me to bring a tape recorder to spring training so he could say that I was working for the station. But really, I was on my honeymoon. It was his gift to me.

Fifteen months after Arlene and I were married, she gave birth to our first child. Patricia Joy was born in July of 1953, and Mark Edwin Milo was born two years later. He was named after both of his grandfathers, and later picked up the nickname "Muggs." Mark used to play in father-and-son games while I was broadcasting for the White Sox. Since Nellie Fox had two daughters, he asked me if my son wanted to be his "son" for the father-and-son game. Mark loved playing in those games, and the players took to calling him "Little Muggs," after Fox, who was nicknamed "Muggs" because of his small stature. The nickname stuck with Mark over the years. In fact, the guys who he went to high school and college with still call him Muggs to this day. Even his mother—and occasionally I—called him Muggs, too.

But he's got to be the tallest Muggs in the world at 6-4. During his senior year of high school football, he weighed 265 pounds. He was a pretty good first baseman and was even drafted in the 16th round by the Braves. He had some power in his bat and terrific

Milo at Chicago's old Comiskey Park in 1965 with his family—wife Arlene, daughter Patricia Joy, and son Mark.

hands. He reminded me of Gil Hodges in that way. He really could field.

As Mark grew up, Arlene was always the team mother in the concession stand and the scorekeeper at all of Mark's games. We were a family of fans. I credit sports with keeping our family together. I've seen some guys in my business where the family didn't care about sports. Often times, they drifted apart. My family took an interest in what I did. In the winter, they'd go to my football and basketball games.

Patty Joy enjoyed dating athletes while in high school, showing off that she could take them to the ballgame and be there with me. She was a big supporter of her brother and me. She got married in

1984 to a man 12 years her senior with four teenage children. So my grandchildren were inherited. And now, I even have seven step *great* grandchildren.

My family is incredibly important to me, especially since Arlene passed away. We would have enjoyed our 53rd wedding anniversary in April 2005, but Arlene died just before I had to leave for spring training. She had been in declining health for a year. The last Sunday of spring training in 2004, she fell in a bathtub and suffered a concussion, which hospitalized her for a while. I had to hire caretakers for her while I was busy working during the 2004 season. When the season was over, I stayed home and cared for her.

Shortly after the first of the year in 2005, I noticed some things wrong with Arlene and called my doctor. She had a brain scan and an MRI that ruled out many things, but did show early signs of Alzheimer's. Shortly thereafter we took her to the hospital to treat a bladder infection. Two days later, our worst fears were realized when Arlene was diagnosed with pneumonia and then suddenly suffered a heart attack. Somehow, the doctors managed to keep her alive long enough for our son and daughter to fly in and say their goodbyes. As a family, we told her, "Mom, if you think it's time to go, you go ahead and go." Late that night, she passed away, in dignity and in peace.

After she passed, a lot of broadcasters called me to offer their condolences. Vin Scully was the first one. The support throughout baseball and from the Astros was fabulous. At her funeral, Phil Garner's father, Drew Garner, a retired minister, and the Astros team chaplain, Gene Pemberton, both spoke on her behalf. And the wife of former Astros pitcher Scipio Spinks sang "In the Garden." In her casket was a deck of cards, as Arlene absolutely loved the game of bridge and became a Silver Life Master. Our honorary pallbearers came from the different eras of Astros baseball: from the 1980s, Nolan Ryan and Billy Doran and from more recent times, Craig Biggio and Jeff Bagwell, and my broadcast partner Alan Ashby.

The experience was comforting for me—and I needed it, since I've had some serious health concerns of my own: leukemia, heart problems, and three back surgeries. Since I lost both my parents to heart attacks, my doctors thought it might be a good idea for me to have a complete physical every year before heading to spring training. I started that in 1961 and haven't yet missed a year. Today, I feel good and I take good care of myself.

I make sure to take great care of my voice, too—for obvious reasons. Some broadcasters use a phony voice to show enthusiasm. It isn't their natural voice that you hear. But when I get excited, it's the real me you're hearing—I don't fake it. Broadcasters can get into trouble misusing their voices, eventually developing polyps on their vocal chords. I've never had that problem because I don't abuse my throat. I keep it real, as they say.

Breathing is important for an announcer, too. My chorus teacher used to preach breathing from the diaphragm, not from the throat. It's worked for me. Despite getting a small cold once in a while, I've never had a sore throat. The saying goes: if you don't have your health, you don't have anything. In my line of work, that's the absolute truth.

B eyond my family and broadcasting, hunting has always been one of my passions. And I've been lucky enough to hunt with some very famous baseball players. But before I share hunting stories with you, let me tell you how I acquired one of my favorite guns, a Winchester .301.

In the early 1970s, Ted Williams was managing the Senators in Pompano Beach, Florida during spring training. I was with the Braves in West Palm Beach that same year, so Ted and I would run into each other once in a while. I was talking to him about bird hunting one day at the batting cage. I asked him for a recommendation on a gun. "All my old pals that I hunt with from Georgia are kidding me because I go quail hunting with the Browning Sweet 16," I told him. "They say I've got to get a .20 gauge over and under."

Ted had signed to be the celebrity spokesman for Sears sporting goods, with the understanding that if they were going to use his name, he had the right to approve everything that they were selling with his name on it. That meant that Ted got to try out Sears' line of guns, too.

"Well, you know," he replied, "I've got a gun with Sears. Winchester makes it for me. It's the Winchester .301, but they stamp my name on it and we sell it at the Sears stores. It's $475." Browning's version of the same gun at that time was about $1,200 to $1,400. So Sears' price sounded better—especially when Ted told me about an upcoming sale.

"The day after Christmas," he said, "in the big ad we put in the paper, there's a one-day sale on the gun. It's a $475 gun and we sell it for one day only for $175. You've got to get it."

The next Christmas, I saw the big Sears advertising page in *The Atlanta Journal-Constitution*. I walked up to the clerk on that sale day and said, "I'm interested in that Ted Williams .20 gauge over and under you've got on sale today." He got it down off the rack and he said, "I want to tell you this gun was made in Japan." Maybe it was the way he said "made in Japan," but I thought to myself, "What if this gun has a defect and they can't get the part to fix it?" I was hesitant, so I didn't buy the gun.

A couple of months later, I ran into Ted during spring training and he asked me, "Did you buy that .20 over and under?" I told him the story of what happened, and boy, did that get Ted upset. He said, "That no good blankety-blank," talking about the clerk. "That gun's not made in Japan. We ship it over there and they *assemble* it. It's cheaper to have them do the work." He continued, "Next Christmas you buy that gun. You'll love it."

The following Christmas, I saw the ad again. Same deal: $175. I went straight over to the Sears store and purchased the gun, and I've taken it on several hunting trips since then. I prefer it to my other guns; there is something about the feel of it, the balance. And there's the knowledge that I got such a great deal on a top-notch gun.

Nolan Ryan and Phil Garner probably top my list of big names that I've hunted alongside. Garner, Ryan, and I did a lot of quail hunting in south Texas around Hebronville and George West and over around Corpus Christi. We hunted on the ranch of one of Ryan's acquaintances, spending several days together and having a great time—that is until Garner ran over the barrel of my gun with his truck. It was repairable, but I never let him forget about it. But Phil and I are longtime friends, and I've forgiven him. I've got a huge painting of Phil and me on a hunting trip hanging up in my home.

Nolan and I also went hunting on the King Ranch, a million-acre spread that is famous not only in Texas but all across the country. How we got there, however, is a good story. A radio station in Corpus Christi ran a contest in which listeners select their favorite Astro. Jose Cruz used to win the contest often because of the huge Latino population in the area. It seemed like he had a lock on the award. But during a season in which the team was rebuilding right after I arrived in Houston, the listeners selected me as their favorite Astro! The radio station hosted a ceremony at home plate before a game and presented me with a big cowboy hat and jacket and a gift certificate for a hunting trip to the world-famous King Ranch. The gift certificate was for two people.

I thought, "Man, oh man, I'm going to go quail hunting on the King Ranch and see all those cattle and all those race horses that they breed." I didn't give a damn about the cap and the jacket, just the gift certificate. It was very nice of the station to be so generous.

As the ceremony finished, I walked toward the dugout, where Ryan was waiting for me. He said, "Don't suppose you got anybody in mind for the guest on that hunt, do you?" And I looked right at him and said, "I'm looking at him." We enjoyed a three-day hunt on the King Ranch. To give you an idea of how big the King Ranch is: once you enter the ranch, it's 65 miles to the next city, which is on the other end of the ranch. There were 75,000 head of cattle on the place the week we were there. Each day, we crossed a 3,000-acre winter wheat field to get to where we were going to hunt.

For me, hunting is a great way to relax. I've never hunted solely for the thrill of the hunt. My rule is that anything I put on the ground will be eaten. I've reached a point where I don't care if I get a lot of birds when I hunt. I just love the activity, and I love watching the dogs. To see a good bird dog work is poetry in motion. The way those dogs have the natural instincts to go on

Milo and his dog are photographed here on a hunting trip with Phil Garner in South Texas.

point. A little puppy eight weeks old doesn't know why he's pointing, but he points. You can develop and nurture that skill and teach the dog to obey or back up another dog on point. I've really enjoyed spending that sort of time with a good dog. I haven't had a bird dog of my own now since 1975, but I used to have four or five at a time.

If I were still hunting today, I would want to hunt over a Brittany spaniel. They're good all-purpose dogs that also make great pets. You can't keep a pointer or a setter in your home because they can't stand the confinement. You've got to have them in a dog run. But you can bring a Brittany into the house. When winter comes and it's hunting season, they go right back out there and they're ready to go.

Unfortunately, my back doctor has warned me, "Your hunting days are over, pal. I don't want you jumping off a jeep or off the back of a pickup truck and landing awkwardly. I don't want you back on my operating table." So, nowadays I enjoy listening to Lance Berkman or Phil Garner or others talk about hunting, but I don't get outdoors to do any myself.

But there's *one* exception that I plan to make. In the 2005 season, Garner told me, "You *have got* to come bird hunting with me this fall." And he wouldn't take no for an answer. As luck would have it, I ran into my back doctor, Rob Parrish, at the ballpark a couple of nights later. I told him that Garner insisted that I accompany him on a hunting trip, and he replied, "Milo, you can go. But there's one stipulation: your back doctor has to go with you."

23

CALLS FROM THE HALLS

I sure have enjoyed my 60 years behind a microphone. And I couldn't be more thrilled to have been recognized for my time spent as a broadcaster. I've spent a good deal of time helping out others. Before the season begins in 2006, I will have helped to raise over $22 million for charitable causes through events that I've either participated in or emceed. I'm very proud of that effort—not from a selfish standpoint, but because I believe that it's essential to give back to the community I'm a part of. That's why it's so humbling to receive an honor from that very same community.

The biggest call of them all came from the Baseball Hall of Fame. My phone rang at one o'clock on a Friday afternoon in the spring of 1992. The person on the other end didn't say hello. But what he did say I'll never forget: "I'd like to speak to the newest member of the Baseball Hall of Fame."

Milo emcees the rally that kicks off the 1988 presidential campaign of George H.W. Bush. Milo later announced Bush's victory on election night.

Those 14 words froze me in my tracks. Goose bumps swelled up on my arms and tears rolled down my cheeks. I've been through a lot during my 60-year career in broadcasting, but this moment was like no other. I was going to join the elite broadcasters— winners of the Ford C. Frick Award—in a special wing of the Baseball Hall of Fame. I would be joining guys like Mel Allen, Red Barber, Ernie Harwell, Jack Buck, and my old partners, Bob Elson and Jack Brickhouse.

Years after they had been inducted, both Elson and Brickhouse both told me, "Milo, there's no doubt about it, you're going to be in Cooperstown with us." Their words were certainly encouraging, but the Frick Award wasn't something that I had ever dreamed of winning. But when Hall of Fame broadcasters begin telling you that they think you'll be joining them some day, it certainly does make one think.

When the phone rang on that fateful Friday, I immediately recognized the voice on the other end. It was Bill Guilfoile, the top publicity man at the Hall of Fame and one of my dear friends for many, many years. He is truly one of the nicest people ever to be associated with baseball. Bill and I were together with the Pirates in the '70s. We had a terrific camaraderie and had kept up with each other over the years. The Hall of Fame felt he was an obvious choice to call me with the good news. Usually the director of the Hall calls the Ford Frick winner, but the director called Bill in and said, "We've selected Milo. Would you like to call him?" I think it meant a lot to Bill that they did that.

Officially, they weren't going to announce their selection until Monday and I was supposed to keep quiet over the weekend. But I had to tell *somebody*. My wife wasn't going to be home till later that afternoon. My son was chomping at the bit, as he thought I had a good chance of being selected. (Personally, I thought it was going to be given to longtime "Voice of the Mets" Bob Murphy.) So, I called my son in Atlanta. He answered the phone, but I didn't respond with a greeting. Instead, I said, "Can you tell me if planes fly from Atlanta to Cooperstown?" He was incredibly joyous, and proud of his father.

The first call I received from anybody in the industry came later that afternoon from Ernie Harwell, who was on the Hall of Fame committee and wanted to congratulate me. The next day, I called Jack Brickhouse to tell him. And then on Monday, the announcement was made to the public.

The response from the Astros was overwhelming: they held a big ceremony for me the night before I left for Cooperstown, and I received a special achievement award at the Houston Baseball Writers Dinner. Then it was off to Cooperstown. The Astro Orbiter boosters chartered a plane and brought 80 people to the ceremony. Many of my friends from Chicago were also in attendance, as were family and friends from my hometown of Fairfield, Iowa. My old roommate from Iowa, Hal Hart, was there, along with an artist named Paul Kline, who had sent me my first fan-mail letter after a record show that I broadcast in 1948. I actually saved that letter and gave it back to him years later.

Because of Cooperstown's proximity to New York, and the induction of former Mets pitcher Tom Seaver as part of my class, the ceremony drew the biggest crowd in its history. So many people wanted to attend—there were a reported 18,000 people there—that the Hall of Fame had to move the ceremony away from the library, where it had always been when the crowd was significantly smaller. In addition to Seaver, pitchers Rollie Fingers and Hal Newhouser were also inducted in 1992.

I was nervous about speaking at the ceremony, because I had never had to respond to such an honor. Plus, a good deal of the audience was not there to support me. I asked Guilfoile for some guidance on how long to talk. He said, "There are no guidelines. It's your moment." Then I asked Bob Broeg, one of my dearest friends, and he told me, "Milo, just remember the crowd is there to hear Seaver and Fingers; they're not there to hear you."

I was receiving mixed messages. The best advice I got, or at least the advice I followed, came from Guilfoile's son, who had just graduated from Notre Dame and had come to work with Rob Matwick in the Astros public relations department. I ran into him one day and said, "I've asked everybody about my speech—except you. You've been with your dad all these years and know about Cooperstown. What should I do?" He responded, "Mr. Hamilton, you're the only one up there who got there by talking, so talk."

I had broadcast for so many teams over the years, that I could not confine my remarks to one town. My speech was long, but there were simply too many people to thank. Brickhouse chose a different route for his induction speech: He said, "People know, in this speech, who I'm thinking of today, so I don't need to mention you by name." I went the other way and mentioned everyone. Johnny Bench chided me about it later. He said, "Man, you really talked." I said, "Who was I going to skip?" But I also livened up my speech by sharing some entertaining stories about my days in the 1950s and 1960s, when I re-created baseball games over the air. Some people told me it was one of the more entertaining speeches they had heard, so I felt like I did all right in the end. If I talked too long, I talked too long. But one thing that I know for certain is that I didn't forget anybody.

Seaver, who preceded me, was rolling along in his speech until he got to his mother, who had passed away. He became emotional, couldn't go on, and had to sit down. I, too, was cruising along in my speech until I mentioned my parents, and welled up. I went on and finished my speech because I was just about through, but knowing what it would have meant for them to have been there choked me up. They both saw me get to the big leagues, but never witnessed any of the great things that happened later in my broadcasting career. I lost my composure, but with no apologies.

I was asked to speak on behalf of the recipients at a dinner held in our honor the night before inductions. Sitting in the front row were Tom and Nancy Seaver, and there had been remarks made about the size of the crowd. I looked right at Tom and said, "Tom, didn't I tell you over the winter that I guaranteed I'd get you a crowd?"

Obviously, he brought the crowd, and the crowd that night at the dinner got a good laugh out of the joke.

B eing inducted into the Radio Hall of Fame was actually more of a surprise than being inducted into the Baseball Hall of Fame. For whatever reason, the Radio Hall does not receive the same exposure as the Baseball Hall. Even I didn't know much about the Radio Hall of Fame, other than the fact that Brickhouse and Buck had been inducted into it.

Before spring training in 2000, Bruce Dumont, who founded the Radio Hall and still heads it up, called to say, "We've just had our board meeting, and we've come up with our candidates for the Radio Hall of Fame this year. We're going to put you on the ballot."

He went through the different categories. They have a pioneer award, which Dr. Bose received, and other awards for personalities, longtime hosts on radio shows, and things like that. There was also an entertainment category, which explains why Bob Hope is in

Astros owner Drayton McLane with Milo at his induction into the Radio Hall of Fame in 2000.

there, along with Jack Benny and George Burns and Gracie Allen. As he was closing the conversation with me, Dumont said, "I just want to wish you well." He added that it's rare when somebody makes it the first year they appear on the ballot.

I figured there would be some voters who wouldn't know me from a bale of hay. I didn't think my chances were good, but I was humbled to even be considered.

But a few months later in August, Dumont called to tell me that I had been inducted in the Radio Hall of Fame. It's hard to argue that it was a bigger honor than the Baseball Hall of Fame, but in some ways it was. The Radio Hall consists of the whole industry, including cornerstones like Edward R. Murrow and Paul Harvey, and there aren't many sports announcers in it. Nine baseball announcers have been inducted, as well as boxing broadcaster Don Dunphy and football broadcaster Bill Stern.

I was elected to a third hall of fame in 1994, the Texas Baseball Hall of Fame. A wide variety of people are in the Texas Baseball Hall, including people who became famous while in Texas and people who were born in Texas and later made the big leagues. There are also executives from the old Texas League days, like Allen Russell, who owned the Houston Buffs, and Solly Hemus, a former big-league player and manager who was arguably the most popular minor-league player in the history of Houston. While Hemus isn't a native Texan, he's there because of things that happened during his career in Texas. Jimmy Wynn is in there, along with Roger Clemens, Jeff Bagwell, and Craig Biggio. Bagwell and Biggio went in together in 2004 and I was the emcee of that affair.

I've certainly put in my time in baseball. Not to mention radio. It means a lot to me to be recognized by my peers and the public for all of my years of service—more than I could ever express in words—even in a book this long.

Being honored by a Hall of Fame is significant and a career-defining experience, but I do prefer receiving acknowledgment from the common fan. From the warm receptions I receive when I attend baseball dinners, caravans, and card shows, it's clear that a lot of fans are appreciative of my efforts on the air. And that means a lot to me. I've known some broadcasters who thought calling a game was only a job. But I love games—first and foremost—and that makes loving my job a piece of cake. Baseball has always been my favorite sport, and I think that shows in my broadcasts. I treat the game with respect and honesty, and it has returned the respect in kind. In 2005, I received another example of that mutual respect, when I was elected into my fourth Hall, the Texas Radio Hall of Fame.

As I head into my 22nd year with the Astros, I realize that I am old—going on 79 years old to be precise. I don't need someone to hit me over the head and say, "The end is near." So, there will be a big change in my work schedule in 2006: I'm only going to do home games, with the exception of a few road trips that I'd like to make. I've thought about it for the last couple of seasons. In 2004, when my wife's health became a constant concern, I thought about hanging it up. I told her I would retire if she wanted me to, but she replied, "No. It means too much to you to keep doing it, and it means too much to me to keep *hearing* you do it."

When the 2005 season reached the halfway point, I decided that I still wanted to be a part of the Houston organization, but only on a part-time basis. Owner Drayton McLane and I worked out an agreement that will allow me to broadcast part-time, but also do public appearances for the team throughout the year. I owe much thanks to many of the folks that I work with for their continued support, including Pam Gardner and my boss, Jamie Hildreth. I will also be eternally grateful to McLane, a man who cares so much about the community, the ballclub, and people like me. We're lucky to have him as an owner.

It's tough to walk away from such a wonderful web of support. But I know that it's time: 55 years broadcasting baseball may not be a record, but it is good enough for me. Still, knowing that it's time doesn't make the process any easier. I got a little choked up after we lost Game 4 to the White Sox, ending our hopes in the 2005 World Series. One of the TV stations had a crew at the game to talk to me about my final game as a full-time announcer. When the postgame show was over, I can tell you unashamedly I had some tears in my eyes. The TV reporter even said, "I think I see some tears." It was a downer at the moment because I really thought we were a better club than what we showed in the Series, but also because I finally realized that I had come to the end of my last full season. It's a tough pill to swallow, and it's not going to get any easier next season when the club goes on its first road trip of the year without me. Still, it is exciting to be in a position to pass on the microphone, so to speak, to Alan Ashby in the same fashion that my mentors, Bob Elson and Jack Brickhouse, passed on the microphone to me.

In the 1970s and '80s, my goal as a broadcaster was to one day be inducted into the Baseball Hall of Fame. Once I went into Cooperstown, my goal was to get to the year 2000, so that I could say that I worked in seven different decades. When I did that and went into the Radio Hall of Fame, I thought, "I'd like to get to a 60th anniversary on the air." That came in 2005, which was my 50th year in the big leagues. My next goal is to make it to 2010, which would give me 65 years on the air and 55 in the big leagues. Those are nice, round numbers to round out my broadcasting career. I'll be 83 in the year 2010, so that goal is going to be dictated by the guy upstairs. Specifically, it'll be up to him as to whether or not my health and my voice hold up. I'm not going to go on the air unless my voice remains well.

My adopted home of Houston has a special place in my heart. From Day One, the people of Houston and the Astros organization itself have been great to me and have made me feel welcome. But I can't let this book go without also mentioning the loyalty of my hometown, Fairfield, Iowa. I return to Fairfield almost every year because I still have great ties there, even though I haven't lived there since 1949. I want the people of Fairfield to know that I don't consider the town just my birthplace—it is still a place that means everything to me.

As does the sport of baseball, and the opportunity that I have had to sit behind a microphone and call a game for the fans. Here's to 60 years, and counting. ...

APPENDIX

MILO AT THE MICROPHONE

Baseball

1950-52	Minor-league team in Quad Cities, Iowa
1953	St. Louis Browns
1954	St. Louis Cardinals
1955-57	Chicago Cubs
1961-65	Chicago White Sox
1966-75	Atlanta Braves
1976-79	Pittsburgh Pirates
1980-84	Chicago Cubs
1985-present	Houston Astros

Other Sports

1948-55	University of Iowa football and basketball
1961-65	Northwestern football and basketball
1961-62	Chicago Zephyrs basketball
1961-65	DePaul University basketball
1966-67	Georgia Tech basketball
1969-71	Ohio State football
1972-73	Georgia Tech football
1980-84	Chicago Bulls basketball
. . . . .	DePaul University basketball
1985-1992	Southwestern Conference basketball

No-Hitters Called By Milo

Year	Pitcher & Club	Score
1953	Bobo Holloman, Browns	6-0

Comment: *First major-league start was only complete game of Holloman's career; wound up 3-7 on the season, his only in the majors.*

1955	Sad Sam Jones, Cubs	4-0

Comment: *First African-American pitcher to record a no-hitter.*

1962	Bill Monbouquette, Red Sox	1-0

Comment: *Rookie stopped 42-year-old Early Wynn's bid for his 300th win—and even had a hit against Wynn.*

1967	Don Wilson, Astros	2-0

Comment: *Ended game by fanning Hank Aaron on three straight fastballs.*

1969	Ken Holtzman, Cubs	3-0

Comment: *Hotlzman recorded zero strikeouts and was aided by a strong wind gusting in from left field.*

1973	Phil Niekro, Braves	9-0

Comment: *His knuckler danced all day.*

1976	John Candelaria, Pirates	2-0

Comment: *The Candy Man survived two early errors in the same inning.*

1986	Mike Scott, Astros	2-0

Comment: *Using his newly developed out-pitch, a splitter, Scott pitched a gem to clinch the NL West crown.*

Year	Pitcher & Club	Score

1993   Darryl Kile, Astros   7-1
Comment: Mets scored on a throwing error by Jeff Bagwell.

1997   F. Cordova & R. Rincon, Pirates   3-0
Comment: First and only extra-inning combined no-hitter. Rincon pitched the 10th and got the win.

2003   R. Oswalt, P. Munro,   8-0
            K. Saarloos, B. Lidge,
            O. Dotel, B. Wagner, Astros
Comment: After Oswalt left with groin injury, five relievers held the Yankees hitless.

INDEX